GW00368048

Escapades

BY THE SAME AUTHOR

non-fiction
JACK THE RIPPER
MARIE LLOYD AND MUSIC HALL
OUT OF STEP
THE MAN WHO WROTE DRACULA
IN PRAISE OF DOGS
A WINDOW ON THE SEA
HENRY: AN APPRECIATION OF HENRY WILLIAMSON
A TRAVELLER IN TURKEY
SOHO IN THE FIFTIES
SACRED MONSTERS

fiction
THE DOG WHO KNEW TOO MUCH
SWANSDOWNE

Escapades

DANIEL FARSON

BLOOMSBURY

ACKNOWLEDGEMENTS

All photographs in this book (apart from those of himself) were taken by Daniel Farson and are his copyright, except for the photograph of beggars in Barcelona which is copyright Hulton-Deutsch Collection.

Daniel Farson's photographs, Gypsy Boy with Dog, and Boy at Barnstable Fair, are available as postcards from Black and Whites Gallery, 50-52 Monmouth Street, London WC2

Grateful acknowledgement is made to the Estate of Bruce Chatwin, Jonathan Cape Ltd and Viking Penguin Inc for permission to quote from *What Am I Doing Here* by Bruce Chatwin (Jonathan Cape, 1989).

First published 1989
Copyright © 1989 by Daniel Farson

Bloomsbury Publishing Ltd, 2 Soho Square, London W1V 5DE

A CIP catalogue for this book
is available from the British Library

ISBN 0-7475-0402-4

10 9 8 7 6 5 4 3 2 1

Designed by Mark Foster
Typeset by SX Composing Ltd, Rayleigh, Essex
Printed in Great Britain by Butler & Tanner, Frome and London

For my friends in Turkey:
Hasan Süzer of the Pera Palas in Istanbul;
Liza and Abidin Kurt with whom I have sailed down the Lycian Coast;
and for Günac Gürkaynak who welcomed me with his usual generosity on my arrival in Antalya;
and for Anthony Eyers in England, the editor of the Oxford magazine, *Isis*, who travels in order to rid himself of his pre-conceptions. He will go far.

For the memory of Bruce Chatwin:

> We will not sleep in the nomad tent, or scale the Minaret of Jam. And we shall lose the tastes — the hot, coarse, bitter bread; the green tea flavoured with cardamoms . . . Nor shall we get back the smell of the beanfields . . . or the whiff of a snow leopard at 14,000 feet . . .
>
> Bruce Chatwin, *What Am I Doing Here*

Beggars in Barcelona – photograph by Daniel Farson
for *Picture Post* in 1951.

Contents

Introduction

'Alman?'

'No. I am an Englishman.'

'You are a group?'

'No, I just look like one.'

These questions dogged me on my journey in the autumn of 1988 to the north-east of Turkey, where I hoped to be a traveller rather than a mere tourist. I was in wistful search of adventure, a rare luxury today when nowhere is remote. The television cameras have stripped the world of mystery and the package tours lead the *hoi polloi* up the slopes of Kathmandu as easily as if it were Primrose Hill.

I am guilty, too, in helping to kill the places I love by writing about them. That is the curse of the travel writer. I tell myself that if I do not draw attention to them, someone else will; also, it seems curmudgeonly not to share my discoveries, but I am wrong. Certain places should be left alone. The trouble is that we can leave nothing alone.

I am an impostor. When referred to as 'a travel writer', I cringe, for 'tourist writer' would be more accurate. I am a bad traveller, as anyone who has accompanied me will confirm. I am impatient; I like my comfort; I hate airports and planes, but do not hesitate to take a taxi if I can afford it. I admire Captain Fred Burnaby who rode on horseback through Asia Minor in the last century, followed by his faithful batman, Radford; and Denis Hills with whom I lunched the day before I left London, who has climbed Mount Ararat *twice*; and I revere my father's attempt, albeit unsuccessful, to cross the Caucasus from the other side, which he described in his book *Caucasian Journey*. My admiration for them, and such intrepid travellers as Dame Freya Stark and Patrick Leigh Fermor, is unreserved, for they went in search of something different – something other than the calculated sameness of popular resorts today with the obligatory Newcastle brown ale. As tourists penetrate every corner of the world, the more everywhere becomes the same.

When I try to emulate the true adventurers, my efforts prove a sham, as this book will reveal. A few years ago I took the train from Istanbul to Lake Van, relishing the prospect of the three-day journey with the chance to find myself again in such enforced seclusion, until I coincided with a friendly English couple, the only other passengers in the tiny restaurant car, who told me they worked in publishing, which prompted the very conversation I was escaping from. We separated in Van, where I booked into a hotel only to find it occupied by an indomitable group of English men and women on a Swan Hellenic culture tour, who told me about the 'unspoilt' corners I was hoping to explore myself. A week later, within the black cobalt walls of Dyabakir, there they were again, greeting each other in high-pitched voices as they settled down for breakfast.

'Oh, not you again!' exclaimed the English lady who was demanding milk with her tea from the harassed Turkish waiter. 'You're certainly following in our footsteps, aren't you!' My euphoria at reaching this astounding south-eastern city evaporated like her milk, which she poured triumphantly – 'When I insist on something, I always get my way.'

On my recent visit to north-east Turkey, the groups were German, and they were everywhere, inducing an irrational resentment. Anyone who has been to a West Country restaurant or hotel when there is a wedding will know that the passing stranger is regarded as a nuisance and is ignored accordingly. The same applies to 'groups', who demand and receive all the attention denied to oneself.

Arriving at my hotel in Erzurum after a twenty-nine-hour journey from Ankara *without* a buffet car, the porter ran out with a gleeful cry of 'Yok!', the favourite negative in Turkey. Before I had a chance to say I had a reservation, he announced that the hotel was full of Germans, though an inferior room was traced eventually and shown to me reluctantly. The restaurant on the top floor was lined with tables prepared for the German invasion, so I headed for the best restaurant in town to find it also in a state of siege. Simmering at a corner table, I decided that of all the groups, the Germans are the most armour-plated in their self-satisfaction, *gemütlich* in their smiling condescension. Expecting the country to adapt to them, the women spread themselves topless on the beaches, to the dismay of older men and the wide-eyed lust of the innocent, younger Turk. In my selfishness, I believed I would be safe in Erzurum, and now a terrible thought struck me: surely they could not be heading for Artvin in the north, my next destination, a town scarcely heard of a few years ago?

I walked across to the young German guide, who greeted me with a disarming smile. 'Yes,' he confirmed, 'we all go to Artvin. You too? So you will be joining us!' 'Is there no escaping you?' I scowled, which was so rude that I went back a few minutes later to apologise. This proved unwise, for the German guide was so gratified that he regarded me as a new-found friend and plied me with *raki*, the lethal Turkish drink known as 'liquid dynamite'. The next morning I discovered a note which someone had slipped into my pocket: 'If you like, we go to public house.' In Erzurum! Who on earth could have written that?

In the afternoon I wondered if my journey was jinxed. The car which was driving me to the Black Sea had crashed in a hideous industrial town called Adapazari, south of Istanbul, and had to be abandoned. The train from Erzurum had developed a fault, so they hammered underneath it at every stop, making the poor thing worse. And now, as the *dolmus* left for Artvin, the steering-wheel came off as we swung into the street.

'Kaput!' the driver explained triumphantly. 'Alman,' he added, pointing to me for the benefit of the other passengers, including a peasant who was already kneeling on his seat praying to Mecca. I appreciated his anxiety. Yet there was another way of looking at it: I walked away from that crash with nothing worse than a bruised knee and jellied nerves; the train reached Erzurum, at last; and if the steering-wheel had failed on one of those knife-edge bends above Lake Tortum, it could have been fatal. I decided that I was lucky.

The Germans were in residence when I arrived at the Hotel Karahan in Artvin, but they looked different. Their loud-voiced arrogance was gone as they munched their dinner in stolid silence. It seemed that something terrible had happened to them (unless it was sheer exhaustion), with the exception of the guide, who waved to me merrily as I sat down with the owner of the hotel, Yavuz Karahan, and a strong young man in uniform whose expression was sapped by sulkiness. Mr Karahan explained that he was the Colonel who had just assumed command of the local military garrison and yearned for his home town of Izmir, which proves that the nastiest places can be missed if that is where you belong.

Unexpectedly, a glass of *raki* arrived on a plate with a message scrawled on a paper napkin, and I recognised the handwriting at once: *Please to drink the health of your Queen.* I was disconcerted, for I had forsaken *raki* for Turkish vodka, but this was a charming gesture which I could hardly refuse. The effect on my companions, however, was extraordinary. Yavuz Karahan wiped his forehead and sighed. 'This is very bad, he has insulted Your Majesty.' He translated the note to the Colonel, who forgot his sulkiness and looked officially grave as he muttered something in Turkish.

Yavuz translated: 'The Colonel asks if you would like to have this man arrested?'

'Oh no.' I blinked. 'I do not think that will be necessary.'

In the awkward pause which followed, my mind began to wander: tomorrow the group would continue on its hectic way and I would be left alone . . . My reverie was broken by the kindly Yavuz, who told me the good news: 'Tomorrow we have English group, so you will be joining?'

Childishly petulant, I frowned, relegated once again to the role of tourist rather than traveller. Then I realised that if I could not beat them, I might as well join, and summoned up a vestige of politeness: 'Of course, I shall be delighted.'

Yavuz smiled but the Colonel looked disappointed, thwarted in his effort to make an arrest. Feeling that my reaction had been inadequate, I asked Yavuz to translate: 'I may go over and sing them a few bars of the *Horst Wessel*.'

Even with the translation, the Colonel had no idea what I was talking about, and nor had I for that matter, but he sensed reprisal and he beamed.

Looking across at the now disgruntled Deutsch, so did I.

Mickey and the Lake

For much of my childhood, I was cast in the role of a suitcase, taken out of the car with the rest of the luggage when we reached somewhere new.

I accepted our nomadic existence as part of the strangeness of life. At the age of eight one is easily contented: a simple game with wooden pegs called 'bolet', played for the prize of a triangular chocolate; a glass of raspberry cordial in Germany; a slice of cake from the great display in one of the *Konditorei*, where the Germans stuffed themselves in the afternoon. These were the highlights of my day.

Conversely, a child is resigned to the moments when the going is bad. Frequently the walls of our bedrooms were spattered with the blood of crushed bedbugs and my mother was one of those unfortunate victims who are attacked by bugs, mosquitoes and insects of every kind. My father and myself remained immune until one wretched room near the Dalmatian coast where the walls appeared to move and we scratched ourselves raw before our budget was abandoned and we fled to the comfort of a 'Grand Hotel'.

Apart from being born with compulsive wanderlust, my father, Negley Farson, worked as a foreign correspondent, which explains our constant travelling. I shared the excitement and suffered only from the absence of another child to make the sharing complete. This was why Mickey mattered so much.

I think it was H. R. Knickerbocker, my father's closest friend and reputedly the highest-paid correspondent in the world, for Hearst, who gave me a large Mickey Mouse, half the size of myself, one Christmas morning when we lived in London, where my father ran the office for the *Chicago Daily News*. 'Red' Knick had a friend at the US Embassy who broke the rules by issuing a passport in Mickey's name, with the relevant

biographical information, and my father supplied a passport photograph. It was a genuine article.

Some officials were unamused. The Belgians tut-tutted, but others joined in the game with a childish delight equal to my own, especially the French, who produced a variety of stamps and insignia pressed down on sealing-wax. The Germans refused to co-operate: 'I think they suspect that Mickey is Jewish,' my mother explained, and, presumably, he was.

My mother had no respect for officialdom and a genuine liking for the Jews. When we booked into a dreary hotel in Magdeburg where the concierge looked displeased at our appearance, she noticed the sign: 'Dogs not admitted. Jews are not wanted.'

'What an unfriendly hotel!' she exclaimed. 'Neither dogs nor Jews?'

'Dogs are allowed on the lead,' he replied uncomfortably.

'And are Jews allowed on the lead as well?' she asked.

With pursed lips he produced a flourish of pink forms to fill in and my mother did so, describing us as 'Dr and Mrs Rosenbaum of Jericho'. I was their son: 'Master Reuben Rosenbaum'.

A curious weakness in my father was his terror of officialdom, almost a subservience, and he growled angrily as we swept upwards in the lift: 'That was a goddamn stupid thing to do. That sense of humour of yours will get us locked up one of these days.' But I was delighted, and though my father leapt nervously at the next knock on the door, it was only room-service, my mother's suspicion that the obligatory forms were never studied was confirmed. In the next hotel she booked us in as Mr and Mrs Featherstone Haugh Haugh Featherstone and Master Nathaniel ditto, of the Tors, Nosham. This was a small, simple hotel where the names and room numbers of the guests were chalked on a large slate, and I felt a twinge of sympathy for the concierge as he inscribed us laboriously as the Famille Featherstone Haugh Haugh Featherstone, leaving little room for the other guests, but the game was on.

In Sweden we blossomed out as Señor and Señora Fernando Alvarez of Chihuahua, Mexico, and Master Ramón Alvarez, but the concierge remained phlegmatic.

'Isn't it sickening?' I said to my mother. 'Who can we be that they won't swallow?'

Accordingly, we celebrated our arrival in Oslo, while my father was looking after our luggage, as 'Mr and Mrs Hirahoto Tagashi of Tokyo', and she was starting to fill me in as 'Master . . .' when the concierge looked past her at my father, who was well known for his books in Norway – 'Welcome, Mr Farson, we have some mail for you.' The game was over, much to my father's relief.

I wonder, wistfully, what happened to Mickey. Last seen, he was sitting in a chair smiling fatuously, his white muzzle a dirty, tattered grey, his limbs threadbare, his day of glory gone.

In my book *Sacred Monsters* I described how our travels were overshadowed by my father's drinking, which isolated me even further. Details were dramas to us, though they mystified outsiders. In my mother's battle to keep him sober, I was enlisted as spy and decoy, running with the latest reports of his progress or collapse, stealing his trousers, searching the room or cabin for the hidden bottle while he slept. On the boat from Sweden I poured salt into every drink brought him on deck by the steward. How long-suffering he was – my father, I mean, though the steward must have found it irksome too. My mother cared so deeply and tried so hard to protect him, yet in doing so she magnified his guilt.

Everything changed when we reached Bohinsko. This was the lake in the far north of Yugoslavia, bordered by Italy and Austria, where we at last unpacked all our luggage rather than the few items needed overnight. In the morning the maid brought us a breakfast of coffee and whipped cream, warm croissants with butter and wild honey, and my father found himself again as he started to write his autobiography on the gravel court-yard outside, thundering on his typewriter in his dressing-gown as Josef, the black-suited waiter, refuelled him with a constant supply of coffee and cigarettes. It is hard to convey the simple enjoyment of the months that followed, but my father came close when he claimed he had found his nirvana as he fished the mountain streams and poached the waters that belonged to Prince Paul, the Regent:

> A short time after I was in the stream my mind was miles away from it, in another world. In this mood, letting my mind wander freely, I had moments

when I was as close to some of the intuitive truths as any Hindu practising Yoga. There was the water, pure as the snows from which it came: the beech and alder in spring bud as the world began to renew itself: the steady rocks ripping the flow into a dancing white rapid: and up above, where the dark pines stood over a deep pool, a bend around which lay another infinitely lovely prospect.

My mother, of course, rejoiced. It cost four shillings a day, for each of us to live there.

I made my secret tree-house in the woods, after perfunctory lessons from my mother, and adopted a piglet in a nearby sty, which looked more skeletal than a pig should look. Regarding the piglet as a substitute for a dog, I brought him scraps of food from the hotel, provided by the courteous Josef. Yet I began to notice something strange: the more I fed the piglet, the leaner he became. One day I looked up and saw the family in fits of laughter. If the crazy English child wanted to feed their pig, why should they bother? From that moment, my generosity, which was really a form of sentimental selfishness, became a genuine responsibility: I pestered Josef for more peelings, until the day when I arrived with my bucket to find that the piglet was gone. That night, as a welcome change from the inevitable veal, pork was on the menu. Probably a coincidence, but I was unable to touch it. Alas poor piglet – beware of pity.

In the spring the lake was swollen by melting mountain snow and I looked down on fields of dark blue, bell-like gentians below the water. My father wrote afterwards that he had never seen such beautiful trout:

> In the swift, icy, bouldered Savitica their backs were a pale mauve. Their spots were vivid scarlet. In the lake itself I once caught one trout, weighing over a kilo, which was darker but must have had a million scarlet spots. He was so beautiful that I wanted to put him back. But he had almost killed himself before he would let me take him.

The source of the River Sava was high in the mountains, broadening out at our end of the lake as it swirled past the private waters of Prince Paul. My father's days of poaching came to a sharp conclusion when he was rash enough to describe them in a London magazine which was brought to the Regent's attention, but he continued to fish there at night and I collected huge bunches of sweet-smelling lily of the valley for our rooms in the hotel – a scent which evokes remembered happiness even now.

In the afternoon, after my father had finished his morning's stint, he fished the lake and moored on the other side where I fetched wood for an open fire and we cooked the fish he had caught a few minutes earlier on a cheap frying-pan in a pound of butter.

Every month or so, we ventured further, climbing to the ski-huts along the snows of the Italian border. I wore the sturdy hobnailed boots made especially for me by the local cobbler, leather lederhosen, and carried a rucksack with my share of the food and drink. We passed fields of munching cows, their bells echoing back as the farmers greeted us with a formal '*Gruss Gott*' or doffed their green hats and wished us '*Dobra dan*'. Then we

started to climb, stopping to drink the pure, cool water of a stream near a painted cross depicting a man lying on the ground – he must have been killed in a fall, or crushed by a tree when he was logging. Crocuses pushed through the thin covering of snow in the lower clearings, and we picked edelweiss to press between the pages of a book. Surprisingly high, we came on lush meadows of bright yellow globe-flowers near the Seven Lakes of different colours, pink, aquamarine, royal blue and bilious green, teeming with water-snakes.

We lost ourselves in snow-fog, which lifted to reveal a group of startled chamois looking down on us. We slept in comfort in the bunks of the mountain hut called Vogel and twitched in the hay of a barn which we were thankful to find one night when we had lost our way. We even climbed Triglav, the highest mountain in Yugoslavia, whose every peak gave promise that the next would be the top, and never was. Underneath a sign which stated that the summit was two hours away, someone had scribbled '*mit Benzin*' and when we reached it at last, the cloud obscured the longed-for panorama of Italy, Austria, and even the Adriatic to the west. A disappointment, but I scratched my name on the metal cone which marked the summit, and coming down we saw a zig-zag line of Italian soldiers on the mountain face opposite, possibly a patrol searching for refugees escaping from Mussolini's regime.

The descent could be hazardous: skidding down a slope with my alpenstock as if I were skiing, I hit a rock concealed by snow and cut myself badly, but it was quick to heal. We burnt in the alpine sun; I picked wild strawberries. Everything tasted good. This was as close to paradise as I shall be.

But by the final summer, the lake was starting to change. In the winter the hotel was empty apart from ourselves, but the summer brought visitors and friends of my father, such as Leo Amery and a fellow journalist, Philip Jordan, with whom he had a professional love-hate relationship. Until now, my father's drinking had been spasmodic, short-lived, unimportant, but with the arrival of Jordan he started to drink with a vengeance in order to compete. After the months of abstinence, the effect was devastating.

Resentment of my mother, all the grievances and frustrations over the years, which had settled in the calm of the lake now rose to the surface. For the most part I was indifferent, able to vanish, until one afternoon when people drank gently on the lawn in the dying sunlight and my father, unusually for him, started to taunt me. A relentless, repetitious bullying began, from which there was no escape, for he held me in a grip as firm as the ancient mariner's. For some reason, possibly those bunches of lily of the valley, he found fault with my lack of courage and dared me to climb an immensely tall pine a few yards away. 'Come on, you think you're so clever, show us what you're made of.' I was too much of a coward *not* to accept the challenge, so I started climbing. It was easy to begin with for the branches were dense. When I reached the top I clung there, suddenly terrified as I glimpsed the commotion below and my mother running across the lawn to join the crowd of people who were watching. Someone cried out: 'Stay where you are – don't worry,' and other messages of alarming reassurance. The tough young swimming instructor who was staying for the summer climbed up the tree and brought me down easily.

The episode was forgotten by the morning. The book was finished at last and the following year – 1936 – it became a best-seller on both sides of the Atlantic, entitled *The Way of a Transgressor*. It was time to leave, and as we drove away we could hear the sounds of hammering: a new hotel was being built.

'The lake will be ruined,' said my mother sadly. My father nodded, and I looked back, wondering how this could be.

They say you should never go back. I chanced my luck in the spring of 1972 when I drove across Europe on my way to the Danube Delta. It was dusk when we crossed the mountains from Austria, deliberately choosing a small road which twisted and turned through drifts of snow, accompanied by the piercing cries of birds apparently peeved by our disturbance. I began to twitch with half-remembered instinct, like that of dogs returning to a previous home in the country, their noses quivering with excitement as they recognise familiar scents. Absurd though it may seem, the *air* evoked the past. Or so I thought.

It was dark when we reached Bohinsko Jezero. At first I could not find the hotel Sv. Janez and, when I did, I realised how memory plays its tricks. Not only was it larger and different, somehow it seemed in the wrong position when I looked out the next day.

As I peered through my shuttered windows my bafflement increased. The view was obscured by morning cloud but I could make out the white-washed church across the river with the faded fresco of St Christopher bearing Christ on his shoulders, as I had seen it so often as a child. However, when I went out to explore, I saw that the hotel was called the Jezero.

The explanation was simple. The modest Sv. Janez where we stayed had been burnt to the ground by partisans in the resistance movement when it was occupied by the Gestapo in 1943. The Jezero was new. The old 'new' hotel a little further along the lake was now one of a dozen hotels, for Bohinsko has become popular as a winter resort.

As the early mists climbed the enclosing mountains, I was startled to find that the lake itself had scarcely changed; it is carefully protected by the government, with new building concealed in the woods. The trout could still be seen in the shallow water reflecting the church, and brought back the sensations of rowing back, heavy lidded, after a blissful day's fishing.

A cable-car whisked me up the mountain-side to the large Ski-Hotel at the top of the Vogel. I glimpsed a chamois on the way, but the trip lacked the exhilaration of climbing to

the top. Back at the Sv. Jezero, I wondered if I could identify the pine tree which my father made me climb that afternoon, and smiled, for there were thousands all the same. And what did it matter!

A German City
in the American Zone

Like a book or piece of music which you fail to appreciate when you're young, yet which catches the heart years later, travel depends on reaching the right place at the right age. When I was eighteen I enlisted in the American Army Air Corps, thanks to my dual-nationality; I was sent to Germany where I proved as unreceptive as a blackboard without the chalk, until I was transferred to the army newspaper *Stars & Stripes* and worked with a hard-drinking group of civilian American expatriates who edited *Weekend*, one of the first of the supplements. The newspaper employed a brilliant German photographer, Hans Hubman, an ebulliently ambitious man who changed sides as quickly as you could butter bread. Rumour claimed that he encouraged his wife to start an affair with the editor; the Americans for their part conveniently forgot that he had been a Nazi. Regarding himself as indispensable, he had no respect for protocol, as I discovered when we covered an officer's wedding. I was so intimidated by the array of brass that I stayed discreetly in the background until Hubman yelled at me across the reception room, interrupting the speech of the best man, who happened to be a general: 'Daniel, if you don't tell this lousy colonel's wife to stop smiling into my camera, I am leaving.' We were arrested instantly and it took a lot of grovelling from our editor, who had to insist that Hubman was mad and did not know what he was saying, before we were released.

Hubman *was* rather mad, but I owe it to him that I became a photographer. He blazed the way with his vast experience and advice, and helped me buy a Rolleiflex (tessar lens) on the black market in Munich in exchange for several cartons of cigarettes.

Munich was covered with a light fall of winter snow as we set off back to the *Stars & Stripes* headquarters in a pleasant village called Pfungstadt, close to Darmstadt. Hubman

was driving our Chevrolet station-wagon, with the German writer, Werner Prym, beside him, and myself sleeping soundly in the back. Next I remember the screams from the front and the hazy realisation that the car was out of control, skidding wildly on the icy surface of the autobahn. On one side lay a valley and a plunge to certain death; towards us in the dark came the lights of a lumbering cortège of circus pantechnicons. It was into these that Hubman had the sense to crash.

When I recovered consciousness a day later, I saw the moving ceiling as I was wheeled into a ward after an operation on a broken humerus, the inappropriate name for a shoulder bone, and various broken ribs. I stayed in that ward for the next few months, the one place in the American army where segregation could not apply. In the bed next to me was a black American called Sammy Roosevelt Mimms, who baffled and alarmed the nice old German nurses by swinging in his cage of wires and pulleys (he had broken both legs). His friends brought him liquid boot polish in the afternoons, which he strained through slices of white bread to extract the pure alcohol.

In the crash one of my front teeth was shattered for ever. In due course the American dentists in the hospital made me a small plate which seemed like an iron glove to start with but was so feather-weight that I scarcely noticed it afterwards. Before this was fixed, I returned to Pfungstadt for a brief visit, tooth-gapped and half my weight. After so many months in bed, for once in my life I looked emaciated. While everyone else seemed genuinely pleased to see me, a middle-aged English woman startled me by her uncharitable welcome – 'You've certainly lost your looks, haven't you! No one will ever find you handsome now' – not that I had ever thought they would.

More irksome than the loss of my tooth was the fact that the Germans from the circus had stripped me while I was unconscious. Possibly assuming that I was done for, they took everything of value, such as my watch, and even removed my uniform. Fortunately, considering how cold it was, a car with Americans found me and took me straight to the hospital at Stuttgart which specialised in bone-cases while the two Germans were taken to a civilian hospital. When Hubman discovered the loss of his tins of sardines, bought on the black market in Munich, he accused Prym of stealing them. 'Yes,' cried the exasperated man, 'unconscious in the dark I searched through the wreckage for your damned sardines and clawed open the tins with my bare hands. They were *delicious*!' Unfortunately Hubman believed this and, weak though he was, he tried to strangle Prym, which convinced the editors of *Weekend* that he really had gone mad at last, until they remembered that he was much the same as before.

Of course the Rolleiflex had gone, though they left the film I had taken in Munich. One of my first visitors from Pfungstadt brought me the contact sheets and I asked for one shot to be enlarged. It showed the centre of the city where dark figures strode anonymously through the slush. It was slightly out of focus, yet I knew instinctively that this was what photography was all about, the antidote to dewdrops on cherry blossom.

The city of Darmstadt was virtually destroyed in the war. One of my photographs reveals a vista of broken, roofless buildings, with the exception of a church on the left.

At first I wondered how people could live there. I underrated their resilience; they led a new type of existence, that was all, and I, too, soon got used to the devastation. It was strange how many of the landmarks remained. In Wiesbaden the cathedral was little more than a skeleton, but it dominated the flattened city. Children played among the twisted iron and piles of rubble; an old man with a stick emerged from a hole in the ground where he lived, and hobbled away in search of food.

By the side of a road leading into the city were small wooden crosses, some with names on them and artificial flowers and fir-cones at their foot. They stood on mounds of brick which once were houses, and the wind blew the dust into my eyes.

Darmstadt in 1947. At first it seemed inconceivable that people continued to live there.

What treasures I might have gleaned on the black market, where Meissen china could be bought for a packet of cigarettes. A sadder waste was the lack of friendship with the Germans. Our uniforms, which we had to wear at all times, kept us apart. I lived in a comfortable world of PX rations, soft foods, ice-cream and warm clothes, in contrast to the destitution surrounding me. Life for the Germans revolved around the black market,

Only a few moments earlier I had seen this man emerge from the hole in the ground where he lived. Such was the desolation of Frankfurt.

with Frankfurt's railway station as the pivot. Every type congregated here, though I was unaware of the undercurrents at the time: youths with long yellow hair; men in shiny black raincoats down to their ankles; men with shaven heads; men in short Bavarian trousers; a few well-dressed men with briefcases under their arms, and the occasional woman. Transactions were hasty. From time to time sirens were heard as American police sped into the square on motor cycles, followed by a German police car into which the offenders were hustled. The crowd, as crowds usually do, looked on delighted by the distraction.

An American army club faced the square and looked down on the scene. A cluster of GIs, white and black in separate groups, stood on the steps staring vacantly at the passers-by, while children watched them hungrily for pop-corn or candy. Above them on the balcony, we sipped at sodas and malted-milks under large umbrellas while the juke-box played inside.

On the outskirts of the city, idly watching a baseball game, a GI played with the massive bulldog that belonged to an officer's wife. He held out a Frankfurter, an irony in such a setting, which the pampered dog licked suspiciously and then dropped. A small boy in a peaked cap walked over, picked it up and started to eat it. His face expressionless.

The relationship between the two nationalities was ambivalent. The GI who gave the dog a sausage looked at the boy indifferently. By the river a group of noisy, happy children were led back from a boat-ride organised by the US 'German Youth Activities', clutching their gifts.

A German secretary bid an effusive goodnight to her American boss. On the way home she told another German girl who worked in the same office that he was an impossible man and they ran down the Americans in general, openly contemptuous of the American lack of culture, laughing shrilly as they exchanged jokes at the Americans' expense. At home, she cut out fashions from American advertisements or read American writers in such magazines as the American-controlled *Heute*. At the mention of Thomas Mann she shook her head sadly, unable to understand why he should have turned against his country and adopted American citizenship. She waited for the American sergeant who was going to take her to an American film, and turned on the American Forces Network on the radio to make the time pass quicker.

A first-sergeant gave us a talk on VD, with alarming anatomical illustrations.

'Why don't you find some decent women?' he asked, and was greeted by humorous shouts of 'Where? There aren't any.'

'Just stop feeding your *Fräuleins*,' he continued, 'and see how long they'd stay with you.'

'Stop feeding your wife, sergeant,' someone called out, 'and see how long she'd stick it.'

Several families shared a house, each had a room crammed with all their possessions. One German family had written to a relative in Chicago, asking him to send for them. Their luggage was packed and they waited for the letter which never came.

A girl downstairs practised music for hours on end; without a piano she sang to gramophone records. Her ambition was to go to America.

An elderly artist painted in his freezing attic, which he used as a studio. An American major returned with his portrait to have his new medal added to the picture.

A German girl due to marry her GI and leave for America in a few days' time hummed happily as she sorted through her belongings, destroying all that was worthless. The baby beside her cried piercingly.

What wistful conquerors we were! Disarming in our innocence, we must have been a mystifying antidote to the goose steps we followed, yet a godsend compared to the untamed Russian soldiers from the east.

Unlike our British counterpart in the ranks, we received good pay, billets, clothes, family allowances, an excellent information system, and the promise of the GI Bill of Rights, which was to send me to Cambridge University after I was demobbed. There was no shortage of volunteers and the GIs who enlisted and landed in Europe were neither embittered nor disillusioned; they were fresh, good-humoured young men still in, or just out of, their teens. In post-war Germany we symbolised youth as we sped everywhere by jeep – no GI liked to walk – flirted with the *Fräuleins*, or *Schatzis*, and spent hours in the barber shop, anointed with after-shave and powder. Cum-Inn snack bars dotted the autobahn, vast advertisements for *Newsweek* covered the back of ruined houses; and Coca-Cola stands heralded the new culture.

Generous by nature, though eager to be liked, the GIs shared their gum with the children and handed round their cigarettes to the old men. Many families existed on their hand-outs. Yet, far from being appreciated, their generosity was taken for granted or despised. In giving so much, their affluence was resented, nowhere more so than in Britain, where the GI was 'over-paid, over-sexed, and over here'. I took a train in England when I was on leave, though still wearing my uniform, and shared a compartment with a tweedy, upper-class couple who spent the entire journey running-down the Americans as crudely and rudely as they could, and for my discomfiture alone, for we were the only passengers. As the train drew into the station, I thanked them in my impeccable English accent for such an unforgettable experience: 'I could not have believed such prejudice existed. You have made me ashamed to be English.' With a smart, military salute, I left them open-mouthed.

Chilled by the English, suspicious of the French, the GIs felt more at home in the American zone of post-war Germany, even if the gratitude was pretence.

In the summer the shabbiness of people's clothes was less obvious and the Germans looked less hungry in the sunlight. But when the winter returned, it was hard to ignore the quietness of the children and the grey, tired faces of their parents. The snow emphasised the bleakness; the ruins had an air of melancholy and were deeply depressing in their permanence.

Yet time has reversed all this. Like so many Occupations, our presence was transitory. I am writing of a half-forgotten past, which seems to bear no relation to myself, nor to West Germany today, which is one of the richest countries on earth.

Life reached its highest pitch at night in the American clubs where German bands played the jazz and jive they had studied laboriously from American records. Their imitation was exact, though some of them must have taken dope to keep going. The clarinettist, eyes closed, mouth open, swaying backwards and forwards, cannot have been older than seventeen. As the band beat out its rhythm, the dancers moved convulsively, their senses almost gone, subordinated to the monotonous, intoxicating and all-embracing sound. The watching GIs beat their feet in unison, their jaws chewing in unison too. As the trumpet screamed the last thrilling notes, the GIs started cheering in a deep-throated roar, louder and louder, shivering in ecstasy.

Marseilles – A Day to Kill

In the army you have the benefit of living with people you might otherwise avoid. At Cambridge I basked in the company of those who shared my enthusiasms. Books and lectures were nothing, friendships everything. One stimulating, humorous friend was called Ozzie and we agreed to spend a summer vacation in Corsica, meeting up in Marseilles beforehand.

Money was short so I booked into a cheap hotel by the station when I arrived with my baggage late at night. This seemed sensible until I woke and realised the full squalor of my room. It was so hot that I was sweating and I lay motionless on the bed for several minutes, as stale as if I had not slept at all. I heard a dog barking forlornly in a courtyard below, someone walking down the corridor in squeaky shoes, and voices in the next room. I guessed it was around nine o'clock.

After a while I swung myself out of bed and filled the stained wash-basin with cold water – there was no hot – and plunged my head into it. The water ran on to the floor and splashed my body, which I dried with a flannel. As I did so, I noticed that directly in front of me there was a small hole in the door leading to the next room. The shutters in my room were closed but light shone through the hole. I tiptoed closer. Two men moved backwards and forwards frequently blocking my view. When their murmuring stopped and the hole grew black, I wondered if an eye was pressed to the other side as well, but after a few moments the whispering started again and the hole was cleared. I caught a glimpse of the bed. One of the men, young, with a sleepy face and thick eyebrows, sat down on it and began counting money, a handbag and wallets beside him.

I looked around for a safe hiding place for my own meagre funds and decided to take my money with me. The men were still counting when I left.

The station was at the top of the hill and I walked down a cascade of steps towards the city. There is something satisfying in striding down a hill, and the din and bustle that greeted me were welcome after that bedroom.

Disappointed to find no message from Oz or his girl-friend at the American Express office, I had the day to kill. I studied the menus outside the restaurants, bought a paper, joined a crowd watching a foreign monarch leave a large hotel, crossed into the 'Quartier Noir' where sunlight caught the shoulders of black troops as they swung their way down the street; I photographed beggars brawling with the police, melting into the scene with the invisibility of youth, in spite of my camera.

After having my hair cut, I sat down at a pavement café in the rue Canebière and ordered the most expensive ice-cream on the list – a *boule de neige*. This was a mad extravagance, but I have never had any compunction about buying myself something marvellous to eat. Even drink comes second to that.

I paid my bill and returned to the American Express office, where the clerk shook his head, so I drifted back to the waterfront. Baby octopuses squirmed around each other in wooden boxes on the boats. I walked on past the harbour restaurants whose proprietors tried to lure me in with deafening shouts, and yielded at last to a small place up some narrow steps, where a radio was playing and a group of sailors were playing cards. I ordered a steak, which was probably horse and cost me less than the ice-cream, and a bottle of wine that cost me more.

Exploring the largely destroyed old district afterwards, dust from the rubble blew into my face, reminding me of Wiesbaden. In the ruins of a church, three boys hooted and danced in front of me.

Those back streets fascinated me. Possibly because I expected no harm, I was safe, yet there was something sinister about them, especially when a midget ran screaming out of one of the houses, up to a group of men in a doorway opposite, who ignored her. Others looked on, hands in pockets, curious yet indifferent, even when she ran from one to another beating her tiny arms against her sides in anguish. A police patrol came quickly up the street, escorted by two graceful Alsatian dogs. At that moment a man dashed out of the woman's house and she pointed at him wildly. Surprisingly, he went directly to the police and she followed, jabbering, trying to beat him with her fists until the police restrained her. The policeman went inside and I asked a man beside me what had happened. 'Her husband,' he explained, making a gesture as if he was stabbing himself in the stomach.

One of the policemen came out and spoke in a whisper, but the woman heard him and a long-drawn-out cry of agony filled the street: '*Il est mort!*' Then the midget buried her face in her hands, weeping convulsively. Onlookers shuffled away uncomfortably, but I stayed until I saw them carry out the body – that of a strong, tall young man.

Out of misguided respect I lowered my camera, and though I wanted to find out more I returned to my dirty hotel. I peered through the hole in the wall to find that the room was empty. The thieves had gone.

Murder in Marseilles: a man directs the police to the house
where the midget's husband has been stabbed.

I relaxed on my bed and chuckled – I had killed my day successfully. Tomorrow I would be sailing to Corsica. But this was not to be. Through some absurd confusion, I continued to call at the American Express office while Ozzie and his girl-friend went to Cook's and finally moved on without me.

After a couple of days, I gave up and took a boat to Tunis, sleeping on deck, staying in youth hostels, exploring – my camera was my constant companion, enhancing everything.

Morocco – Bombs and Busts

The police were putting up road-blocks as we entered Marrakesh. Unaware of the reason, I was excited by the prospect of the city which Churchill called 'the Paris of the Sahara'. I expected glimmering rose-pink walls rising from a stony plain, palm trees swaying in the foreground and snow peaks in the distance. That is what I eventually found, but we came by a back way into a drab main street lined with European houses, and it was drizzling too. Churchill's comparison seemed grotesque.

The sense of anticlimax changed abruptly as we crawled along the narrow souks of the 'native quarter'. There was an atmosphere of hysteria which we understood when we learned the reason for the road-blocks, preventing anyone from leaving the city. Only an hour earlier the Sultan had staggered out of a mosque clutching his face, blood splattering his jellaba. The Glaoui, one of the last feudal warlords of Africa, charged outside like a bull, seized a carbine from a soldier and shot the escaping assassin four times through the head, with startling agility for a man who was probably in his eighties.

A bomb had been thrown while everyone was prostrate in prayer. The Glaoui, as host, was angry and mortified, and ordered the immediate execution of other suspects. However, the rumour was permeating the alleys of Marrakesh that the Glaoui wished to silence his accomplices before they could blab – hence the consternation when we reached the great main square, the cauldron for all the gossip of Morocco.

I saw the Glaoui the next evening, a rare privilege accorded to the reputable journalist I was with, after months of diplomatic negotiation. The Glaoui had seldom been photographed before, except on a public occasion, and lived in such seclusion that he was scarcely known to the outside world, though he had played host to Winston Churchill at the luxurious Mamounia Hotel where Churchill, never averse to a free meal, unpacked his canvases and painted his scenes of Morocco.

In spite of his wealth, which rivalled that of the Sultan himself, the Glaoui lived in stark simplicity, which made the two cheap busts of Churchill with holes where the small, imitation cigars had been, and a signed photograph of Churchill and Stalin, look especially incongruous. A number of clocks told different times, but chimed cheerfully in unison; a toy tank and a toy plane rested on the mantelpiece.

Impassive, his boredom apparent, the Glaoui received us without acknowledgement. He spoke French but preferred to use an interpreter, presumably to gain an advantage during the interview. His face and brown-striped jellaba would have merged with those of the crowd, but his eyes made me realise he need only lift a finger to have us killed; I wondered how many had died because they had offended him. Few men have scared me more.

Possibly my nervousness infected my Rolleiflex, which jammed in fright. Like a hunter trying to re-load his rifle as the lion charged, I struggled with a new film. Having missed the assassination attempt, I saw another priceless opportunity slip away. One photograph did come out, although I continued to click away in the hope of looking competent. I over-compensated for this failure during the next few days by photographing everything in sight – goats in trees, blind beggars, boys on horseback, dancing girls, and the great square known as Djemaa el-Fna, which means Congregation of the Departed, named after the decapitated heads which once surrounded it.

The great square of Djemaa el-Fna in the heart of Marrakesh,
a maelstrom of nationalities and intrigue.

Hoping for a further assassination attempt, I went to the Sultan's Palace the next morning to witness his hurried departure for Rabat. Soldiers lined the courtyard while armed servants emerged carrying baskets of food and briefcases. A murmur ran through the crowd as the aged Glaoui arrived, stepping shakily from his Bentley. An eye-specialist hurried inside. Then the Grand Vizier, reputedly 103 to 112 years old, ambassador to Madrid around 1870, hobbled into an inner courtyard where he sat down to rest.

Suddenly the Sultan emerged, the cotton-wool plainly visible behind his dark-glasses. I thought how unnerving it must be to be plucked from comparative obscurity at the age of seventy-five to become the target for political assassins. The cortège set off: men with rifles were silhouetted on the rooftops until we left the narrow streets and saw the

How intently the boy with the bicycle listens to the lamentations
of a blind beggar in the square at Marrakesh.

snow mountains in the distance. The sun blazed down and at last the city looked as it
should – red-hot. The wider road was lined with chanting, though hardly enthusiastic,
crowds and guards flanked the route all the way, standing hundreds of yards deep. At
the station there was a token guard of honour to celebrate the Sultan's ill-fated visit, with
flags and a goat with gilded horns. Inscrutable expressions from the Sultan, the Glaoui
and the French general D'Hauteville, who resembled an Englishman, as their national
anthems were played by the band. There were tears from the venerable Grand Vizier

A corrugated mosque in the shanty town of Bidenville
on the outskirts of Casablanca.

although it was hard to tell if these were due to fatigue or emotion. Certainly the crowds seemed unmoved, but the old Sultan had reigned for a long time and when I met Berbers in the Atlas Mountains the following week, many did not know that the old Sultan had been replaced by the new.

With the Sultan safely on his way, I returned to that extraordinary square, so vast it covers 1,500 square yards, and spent hour after hour there. Eventually I blended into the seething crowds and was able to photograph without attracting an entourage of beggars beseeching baksheesh.

The far side of the square was enclosed by a line of horse-drawn carriages with the covered souks behind them. On the other side I entered an entire street of barbers who were shaving their customers' heads or performing such operations as blood-letting. Steam rose from the ragged tents of food-stalls, smelling of sheep's entrails, and I caught sight of massive dishes piled with fried locusts, mutton in oil, or couscous. Splashes of colour everywhere, among the antheap activity: a stall of oranges caught by the late-afternoon sun; the costumes of those who came to town – Arabs, Berbers from the desert, and Sleuhs from the mountains, who wandered as fascinated and delighted as myself among the attractions. The range of skin-tone and feature was remarkable, including the Blue Men from the far south.

The Sleuh dancers, effeminate-looking boys in flowing white costumes and small black caps, danced rhythmically, taking small, restrained steps, shaking, always expressionless. Tumblers leapt in the air, the piteous wail from a group of blind beggars struck the ear unpleasantly.

A large, impassive crowd sat listening intently to the story-teller who recalled an episode in Moorish history. A fire-eater kindled the end of his stick in the ashes at his feet, plunged it into his mouth, withdrew it and belched forth smoke. The snake-charmer with long, matted hair, thrust the head of the snake into his mouth, wound it round his neck, then shook his hand violently pretending he had been bitten. The crowd laughed, especially when he spotted my camera and hung the snake around my neck. It looked as alarmed as I did.

And beyond the hubbub in a quiet, inconspicuous corner I found the medicine men. They squatted mysteriously behind powders and pills and bottles, skins of lizards, rams' heads, teeth, feathers, eggs, red-pepper and the hearts of snakes. Could I have mistaken the latter – do snakes have hearts? The medicine men struck me as entertaining actors, but the Moors still had faith in their powers, regarding them as true magicians. There was, I learnt, a great demand for aphrodisiacs, and they had bottles capable of providing the strength for a night of orgy. Equally, they were consulted over marriages and childbirth, and bridegrooms came to them for oil and raw eggs before their wedding night. Veiled women anxious to gain power over their husbands or lovers bought potions, the efficacy of the spell largely depending on the cost. The credulous victim usually succumbed, until he found an antidote which was stronger and more expensive.

The sacrifice of animals was an essential part of the cure, though I could not grieve for the ants who were placed over an open wound, plunging their claws into the skin to pull the edges of the wound together. Then the back of the ant was removed.

I was warned that Marrakesh was an 'immoral' town, but did not have the experience to find it so, though the turbulence of the square suggested an undertow of eyes watching and schemes hatching and aphrodisiacs starting to itch. How flirtatious the eyes

behind the veils; how determined the cavalcade of men heading for the Quartier Réservé set aside for prostitutes.

All the excitement I needed was offered by the pageant of the square, heightened by the drums of the Senegalese which beat incessantly. At seven, when the sky glowed before the sudden fall of night and swallows dipped and dived over the rooftops, I climbed to the top of the Café de Paris, my mouth parched, and ordered mint tea, which was brought in a shiny oriental teapot made in Sheffield. As I sipped this incomparable drink, both sweet and refreshing, I looked down on the stage I had left, trying to discern the characters, and then looked the other way towards the snow mountains shivering beyond the city, turning from gold to pink and fleeting red. I cannot remember if I saw such details, but I recall the contrast between the desert and the thousands of palms, olive and orange trees, and cyprus rising slenderly above. Even a freak green golf-course had been conjured from the sand by constant flooding, paid for by the Glaoui, who allowed the Europeans to play there free.

It was dark when I descended. A child caught hold of my arm and ran beside me begging in a plaintive whine. I paused before a French café wondering if I should have a drink before dinner, when there was a shattering explosion inside. Instantly, Moroccans from the souks converged and pushed me forward. I clung to my camera. Moroccan police with wooden sticks beat us back, so it was hard to see what damage had been done apart from the inevitable broken glass. Several people were taken to the chemist next door, bleeding profusely. Among the wounded was the English writer, Peter Mayne, who had just enjoyed a literary success with *The Alleys of Marrakesh* and who later became a friend in Athens – a charming, humorous man. He had seen the bomb flying over him, and ducked. The French police arrived, enraged because they patronised the café and the bomb was plainly intended for one of them. An ambulance took Peter Mayne to hospital, the crowd jostling the stretcher. Then the square was peaceful for the first time that day.

I left Marrakesh at six the next morning. A soldier was violently sick on the tracks as I waited for the train, and people at the buffet wore the hopeless air of early morning.

Around the World with a Mop

Soho was growing stale and I was ripe for new experience. I decided to join the Merchant Navy, and thought romantically in terms of a rusty tramp limping down the coast of South America, leaning over the rails to watch the firework sunsets exploding over a molten sea. The reality was closer to a floating hotel, and a strange hotel at that.

I quickly realised that joining the British Merchant Navy was a formidable undertaking. With conscription, you had little alternative but accede gracefully. This was different: others may have joined up for the security, but I was acting on impulse. I knew no one already in the Merchant Navy. My father protested that it would be a waste. 'Don't you think it's time you got somewhere in life?' And my mother sighed and thought it 'a pity'. My Soho friends were equally discouraging: 'You won't enjoy it,' 'Poor you!' and, mainly, 'But *why?*'

The reason seemed obvious to me – the opportunity to travel and the vital change of scene – but I had no idea how to set about it. Someone told me that the Norwegian Merchant Navy would take anyone, and this was confirmed when I telephoned their embassy. 'No, you do not need experience, but you've got to be under sixteen. Are you under sixteen?' I put the phone down.

The shipping line for South America had its offices in Liverpool, so I called at its agent in the City of London. The official was sympathetic, but doubted if he could help. I was trapped by the familiar stalemate: without a union book I could not go to sea, and I could not get a union book unless I had experience. As an afterthought, he asked what I had been doing.

'That's perfect!' he exclaimed when I told him. 'Come as a ship's photographer, we can arrange that easily and you won't have to go through the pool.'

When I told him I was sick of photography, which was why I wanted to escape, he shook his head hopelessly and told me I had come to the wrong place anyhow: if I was determined, I should try the docks where the men signed on.

With the indefatigability of youth, I headed east, changing buses and trudging over interminable cobblestones past lines of tantalising ships, until I reached the office where I was told that I did not have a chance without a book: 'On a liner it wouldn't matter so much, one dud among so many would hardly be noticed. But on a small ship, one weak link can be serious.' He flashed me a false smile and it was stalemate again.

It is one of the surprises of life that if you want something badly enough, you can normally get it. The next day I tried to join the union at the Shipping Federation, where an official looked me up and down as if I had done him some personal grievance.

'How old are you?' said the official, sighing contemptuously when I told him I was twenty-eight. I *might* get a job as a night-watchman or fireman, *if* I took a course, but he did not think it likely.

Feeling older that God, I tried my luck at the pool, where the scene resembled a stage-set for a musical. Colourful figures lounged around the room and coloured seamen with white T-shirts and black leather jackets lined up before the iron grilles. With the kindness of strangers, and of seamen in particular, they told me what to do, but when my name was called it was stalemate yet again – they could not give me a book unless I had been signed on by a shipping line. As I trudged back along the cobbles, a young man ran after me with the name of a line that needed men at that moment, but when I phoned I was told there were no more vacancies. I was applying at the start of the summer, when everyone wished to sail. Before Christmas, when seamen wanted to stay ashore, it might be different.

So I returned to Soho. And it was there that Francis Bacon gave me unexpected support by contacting one of his patrons, who happened to be the director of the Orient Line, and one word from his secretary secured me an appointment at Tilbury with the catering superintendent. Less glamorous than joining as a deckhand, but I was prepared to accept anything by now. Inevitably, it was not as simple as that.

The superintendent was a genial man in a hurry. He caught me off guard by offering me a job on a short trip as a letter-bureau attendant in the purser's office. I did not have the nerve to refuse and was handed a form to take to the doctor. After weeks of trying, I had been accepted in a matter of seconds, and, far from being elated, I felt a certain disappointment. To my relief, the doctor was out at lunch so I walked to the bustling pub that lay in the centre of the ramp linking the liners and the Tilbury trains.

Three extraordinary figures minced towards me, with bouffant hair-styles and make-up, chattering like monkeys, although they paused to whisper and ogle as they passed. Each man was over six feet tall, and I was as surprised by this apparition as Macbeth by the witches. At the age of twenty-eight, my naïvety was absurd. I had no conception that in the tradition of the Navy – described by Winston Churchill as drink, sodomy and the lash – 'screaming queens' like these were as essential to life on a liner as sherry to a trifle.

A liner had just docked and a group of stewards were having a drink in the pub. I had the pluck to ask for their advice which they gave with surprising generosity. Exactly as I feared, the 'cushy' job I had accepted would be neither that of crew nor passenger, and would not even count as the 'experience' demanded by the union. I hurried back to the docks and intercepted the superintendent as he was leaving. By now he realised I had no influence 'high-up' and viewed my return impatiently.

'Very well,' he said abruptly when I asked to join as an ordinary deckhand or steward, 'but there are no vacancies left, unless you're prepared to sail as utility steward on another ship.' I had no idea what this meant but accepted instantly. On the train back to London, I shared a carriage with two Australian deckhands from the ship I was due to sail on in a week's time. 'It's rough,' they said. 'Couldn't believe it first night out, all these birds sitting round the Pig and Whistle, only they weren't girls but stewards dressed up, camping their heads off. Never speak to them; once you do they won't leave you alone.'

The other Australian agreed: 'They stopped bothering me when I threatened to thump them.' All this was very surprising. 'And what,' I asked, 'is a utility steward?'

'The lowest of the low,' they replied. 'You can't get lower than that.'

Three days later I was passed by the doctor, though I needed a cup of tea at a nearby buffet before I could provide a specimen, and was duly accepted by the union after paying three guineas membership. I was pleased by the 'guineas', like joining a club. I was handed my book and cards and emerged from the office as a seaman at last.

The S.S. *Orcades* lay by the quayside like a stranded leviathan. From a distance she appeared to be held by Lilliputian threads, which proved to be gigantic ropes close to. She weighed 30,000 tons, a great dead object though the parasitical life surrounding her was hectic. Food and stores poured into the holes that gaped in her side, cranes lowered cargo into her depths, and a constant insectivorous stream of tiny figures hurried up and down the gangways. The crew totalled a staggering 634: waiters, bedroom stewards, deckhands, engineers, officers and clerical staff. At the lowest level, beneath contempt, were the utility stewards, the U-gang. Mistaking my instructions, I thought my rank was second steward, which earned me odd glances as I found my way through the labyrinth of steel corridors and stairs, laden with my kit-bag and uniform of white jacket and blue trousers, which I bought in the store that morning.

A closer look at my chit revealed that I should report *to* the second steward, who proved the most powerful man in my new universe. A hierarchy of power saturated the ship, with the captain at the top and myself at the bottom. The second steward was a large man with cunning eyes and, though he was hardly older than myself, he called me 'laddie' when I at last found his cabin.

'Yes?'

I handed him the chit: 'Could you tell me what cabin I'll be in?' As an afterthought, I added 'sir' but this did not appease his temper.

'Look here, laddie,' he told me, leaning forward, 'don't bother me about your cabin. I've more important things to do than think about your cabin. I'll see about that later, if I have time. Now I'm going to lunch. You don't *want* to make me late for lunch, do you?'

In the Pig and Whistle on the S.S. *Orcades* with a French Impressionist behind us.

He waited.

'No, sir,' I replied cravenly.

'That's right, laddie.'

Emboldened, I asked where I should leave my kit, and his fleeting smile vanished as he glanced at my duffel bag and the typewriter beside it. 'Not here,' he snapped. 'Don't let me catch you leaving it here.'

His own steward, a Scottish boy of sixteen, offered to take me to the crew's quarters when he had left. After climbing down numerous companionways, I entered the iron jungle that was now my home. The floor was strewn with litter, pipes hung overhead, it was dark and hot. Seeing my dismay, the boy tried to cheer me up: 'Don't mind him. It takes him an hour to shave each morning.'

'Why?' I asked, innocently.

'Because he's two-faced.' With that he left me, and I tried to return to the gangway. It took days before I knew what deck I was on, months before I found my way easily.

Back in the pub on the ramp, a member of the crew urged me not to sail as a utility steward: 'Anything else. Go for engineer's steward. You can easily fake a reference. Sneak into some London hotel tonight and steal a sheet of their notepaper, and get someone to write on it for you. They never bother to check up.'

By now I had accepted my fate in the U-gang and was not going to risk subterfuge. I was so elated at being in the Merchant Navy at last that I scarcely noticed the squalor of my cabin when I returned in the afternoon. There were eight of us in the space of a train compartment, and every inch was precious. The best bunks were taken so I put my bag on the lower bunk in the centre, regretting the refuge of a corner. A young man was unpacking, then an Irishman came in who seemed pleasant enough, followed by an owlish, balding, middle-aged man.

'Where you from?' he asked thickly.

'London,' and his face lit up with astonishment.

'A Londoner!' he exclaimed, as if I had said, 'Paris. France.' 'Why, I'm from London too.' Plainly I had forged a bond.

Then Squeezy joined us, a cockney boy with a broken tooth, which gave him a disarmingly crooked smile. He spoke with a Dickensian East End accent, as if his mouth was full of hot chestnuts, and he didn't know what to make of me.

Squeezy and I were ordered to scrub a corridor by the assistant second steward. It sounded pointless but simple. Squeezy shrugged indifferently: 'C'mon, we'll get a bucket.' Nowhere could we find a spare one. Those who possessed such an article were determined not to lend it, so we returned to the assistant second steward who pointed to his watch impatiently: 'You've been an hour on this job already. Get a move on.'

'Can't,' Squeezy scowled. 'Can't get a bucket, can we?'

'I don't care about that. Get that work done. I've more as soon as that's finished.'

With the nonchalance of a seasoned traveller, Squeezy was unmoved. As soon as the assistant second moved on, he suggested we go to tea, and I tagged along clutching the mop I had found in a broom cupboard and refused to part with.

In the galley, large and impersonal, Squeezy started a filthy conversation with a greasy man who smiled cruelly. He wore a white cap on the back of his head and wielded a cleaver which he used to emphasise his points. He was the butcher and he relished his domination of the younger stewards. Squeezy did not have his heart in the search for buckets, but I was anxious to get the job finished and go ashore for a final night in London. I returned to the bucket-locker and in my best Cambridge accent spoke in a tone unused to disagreement: 'Please, I must ask you to let me have two buckets.' Taken by surprise, the bucket-steward handed them over as a special favour, on condition that we returned them within the hour.

Scrubbing a floor can be soothing, but in this case, as in so many others, the job was created for the sake of it: a flow of people walked past and over me, leaving a trail of black footprints that had to be cleaned again. When we had finished, I found the second steward and explained my wish to go to London.

'So do I, laddie.' He laughed. 'I'd like to be able to leave my job just like that and say goodbye to my family, but I've work to do.' I stood in hangdog pose, servile and silent, suspecting, rightly, that this was a game of bluff. 'Do you need him?' he asked the assistant second, who hesitated for a moment, for the sake of conviction.

'No, I guess I can keep Squeezy on the job. I guess I can spare him.'

'Right then, report at six in the morning and mind you're there.'

Ignoring a fearful scowl from Squeezy, I hurried out of the dock and was promptly arrested. The evidence looked damning. I was carrying my unlikely typewriter, with my Rolleiflex over my shoulder, and by chance such a camera had been reported stolen. The more I explained, the more damning it sounded. I protested that I needed the typewriter to finish an article on Big Ben for the *Evening Standard*, and the Rollei to photograph Dean Martin and Jerry Lewis who were rehearsing at the London Palladium. Improbable though it sounded, these were my last two assignments before I sailed and I needed the money badly.

That night there was an unsettling incident at the White Tower, where a friend took me for a last supper. Plainly, the swarthy young man at the next table had come in by mistake, as he realised when he looked at the prices on the menu. Increasingly embarrassed, he complained loudly to the Greek waiters. They explained later that he was a Greek waiter himself, on his night off, homesick for good Greek food, but unaware that the White Tower was one of the most expensive restaurants in town. Touchingly, the other waiters were distressed on his behalf and did their best to avoid a nasty scene. The manager was sent for and assessed the situation at a glance. With superb politeness he disarmed the young man by offering him a drink on the house, and then suggested he should leave, speaking with the undisputed authority of manager to waiter. The look of angry humiliation on the young man's face was particularly disturbing for me. Often I had been in a restaurant and heard the crashes and cries from harassed waiters behind the swing-doors of the kitchen. Within a few hours, I would be on the other side of the swing-doors myself.

I was appalled by my first glimpse of the plate-house after the ship's muster at 6.30 the next morning. The entire ship's company had filed past the captain and the directors of the line as our names were checked off the list with unsmiling stares – a nervous moment, echoing the first days at school and enlistment in the army. My pristine blue trousers and starched white jacket were then abandoned for jeans and white T-shirt, though even this was over-dressed for the steamy heat of the plate-house. The din, as I took my place, was hideous. Trays of silver emptied with a crash, waiters raced past, throwing us the dirty plates; we scraped off the scraps with our fingers into the vast garbage cans, hurled the plates into an ancient washing machine, where they revolved crazily in murky water, and then piled them into wooden racks which were lowered into boiling water. After drying and stacking them, we carried the molten piles of polished plates to the parts of the galley where they were needed. Scalding silver-plate was an additional torture.

This first impression was a parody of hell, with half-naked, sweating figures glimpsed through the clouds of steam – all it needed was the crack of a whip. In fact the operation was run with the efficiency of a conveyor-belt and monotony was the worst of it. At the end of that first lunch, however, my hands were shrivelled from the hot water like the skin of an embryo in a bottle.

What did that matter! The *Orcades* was moving! And as soon as the last plate was stacked and I was released, I hurried on deck and leant over the rails. As we made the slow passage out of port small figures on the shore waved goodbye interminably. Soon we were out in the mouth of the river passing among other liners, tankers and yachts.

I gazed entranced, growing a new skin in the keen fresh air. When we left land and thrust our way into the open sea, I felt absolute relief. My camera had been left in

London. No telephone to answer, no responsibilities except duties on board, nothing in pursuit and everything ahead of me as we started our voyage around the world.

'My God, you did right!' I told myself.

It was one of the best moments of my life.

Travel is freedom! It does not matter if there are moments of discomfort or even of disaster, these are frequently the memories which give the greatest pleasure. Change is the vital factor, the chance of something different. Above all, there is the advantage of seeing yourself in a different light. 'Finding myself' in a different place was certainly true of the *Orcades*, where wealth (not that we had it), age or background were irrelevant. Squeezy confided in me: 'I fought you was educated when I first saw you, didn't I? But it's all right now I know you're not.' He gave me a crooked leer as he paid me the compliment.

On board ship I had to be myself, with only my wits to support me. There was no question of 'pulling rank', for I had no rank to pull, though I discovered that the life of a liner depended on a process of bartering. It permeated the whole ship until you reached the level of the U-gang, where there was nothing left to barter with.

I was lucky. The second steward was more sympathetic than his appearance suggested, and later that first afternoon his assistant told me that I was being transferred to the fruit locker.

'It's a good job,' he assured me when I looked bewildered. 'Bags of overtime.' Overtime was the last thing I needed; undertime would have been preferable: my hours in the fruit locker were 6.30 to 10.00 a.m., 12.30 to 3.00, and 5.00 to 10.00 p.m. – an eleven-hour day, seven days a week. But I had escaped from the monotony of the plate-house and even the pathetic rate of overtime proved a welcome addition to my pay-packet of £26 10s 10d. a month, much of which was consumed by taxes, laundry and clothing. Now I received an extra 3s 6d. for every hour over ten hours. Better still, I had the fruit to barter with and was now a part of the ship's pecking order.

When I told the others that I was being elevated to the fruit locker, it touched me that they felt no resentment. 'That's a cushy number,' said the Irishman generously; he was left in the steaming plate-house.

I never found it that cushy. On the first evening there was pandemonium as an angry surge of 'wingers' formed in front of my locker, shouting for pineapple and melon. I had to cut the tops off the pineapples and barrel out the flesh with an empty tin, which sounds easy enough except that pineapples come in different shapes and sizes, while the tin remained the same. Then I had to cut the flesh into slices, restore them to the shell and crown them with the green, plumed top. Fun for a dinner-party, hell when I had to cope with several hundred pineapples in a matter of minutes, with the waiters growing angrier by the second.

To my surprise, the second steward came to the rescue. Far from complaining about my clumsiness, he stripped off his braided jacket and subdued the wingers into sullen silence. Though it was alarming for me, panic in the galley on the first night at sea was nothing new.

Having relished fruit, I began to hate it. Crates of oranges, grapefruit and apples had to be carried from the stores, with hundreds of melons to slice and gallons of fruit juice to pour – and this was only for breakfast. I cursed the passengers who insisted on fresh orange juice, though I should have done the same. Mangoes proved especially tiresome. They were mostly unripe and looked dirty the moment they were cut, and it was only at Fiji where they were fresh that I realised how perfect they can be. Those damned pine-apples were the worst with their acid juice burning into the cuts in my raw fingers. I heard disturbing reports of my predecessor, who had refused to return, preferring to swelter in the tropical depths of the laundry room. He suffered from such a bad case of scabs from the pineapples on the last cruise that his face had to be covered with a blue ointment. I looked at myself anxiously each morning, yet seemed much the same. In fact there was little time to bother about appearances; at night I collapsed on my bunk and plunged into a dreamless, limitless sleep until I was roused at 5.30.

Gradually the pressures eased and the haze of those first impressions began to clear. Even the plate-house seemed less of an inferno when I was sent there to help out, and the smells from the galley were hardly noticeable. Since childhood, I have been fasti-dious over food: rice puddings make me gag, greasy fried eggs give me nausea, so I dreaded the prospect of hundreds of fried eggs bubbling in lakes of hot fat for the crew's breakfast. I failed to realise that in such conditions the galley has to be pristine, venti-lated, hosed down after every meal, inspected every day, more hygienic than any restaurant kitchen I had seen. Down in these depths there was no sensation of being on a ship. There was virtually no roll, which I was glad of when I emptied the refuse through the gaping chute in the side. Once, carrying a perilous pile of crates, I slipped on some rotten fruit and teetered on the edge. 'The slightest heave and I'd be overboard!' I re-marked to the second steward, who surveyed me impassively.

'They would stop and pick me up?' I added as an afterthought.

'Hardly worth it, laddie.' He smiled. 'You'd be sucked straight into the props.'

I learnt cunning as I adapted to the life as a cog in the thousand-odd rackets on board. My perquisite as King of the Fruit Locker was being able to grant favours and thus re-ceive them. I did not have time to sit down in the crew's mess so I ate the same food as the passengers – an accepted though forbidden practice. In return for supplies of fruit and tins of juice, favoured waiters allowed me to choose from the First Class menu and added the dishes to the passengers' order. As the waiter arrived for fruit, he rested his tray for a moment and a plate of crayfish or chicken vanished below my counter. I dined on steak and baked Alaska; the only thing missing was the wine. If the chief or second steward passed by at the crucial moment of exchange, the waiter simply asked for the fruit and continued with my 'order' into the passengers' saloon, delivering it on his way back when the danger had passed. When I had a rare moment to myself, I would dive below the counter, swallow a mouthful and reappear. I mastered the trick of holding the food motionless in my mouth while speaking, in moments of crisis. For the next few months I never sat down to a meal and ate all the food with my fingers. My table-manners have never recovered.

In such confined conditions we had to be scrupulously honest with each other, so nothing was borrowed without being returned. The shipping line, however, was considered fair game, and I expect they knew it, for the graft provided incentive for everyone, from the chief steward to the youngest laundry boy. Invariably there was some favour which could be returned, and many an engineer or deckhand in the furthest corners of the ship would be handed the menu for the evening, served every course by a steward who would then be 'seen all right' in some capacity or other.

Greedy since birth, my enjoyment in the food was so obvious that waiters took pleasure in recommending the best dishes of the day. Conversely, they hated the 'bloods', as the passengers were called, though they lived in expectation of their tips. The benefactors they resented most were the Australian and American passengers who consumed staggering amounts and were constantly asking for more.

A Greek waiter complained to me bitterly: 'This man, he eats like an 'orse. He starts with melon, then homlette, then melon again, then he things he wants anudder homlette before the main course – oh my God!'

For my part I began to hate the woman who insisted on bottled ginger with every meal even though it wasn't on the menu, for special orders like this meant a dash to the stores below while the waiters were kept waiting. A simple complaint to the chief or second steward meant passengers could indulge their whims, but retaliations were intricate and sweet. One legendary incident involved an arrogant lady passenger who insisted on pissing into a chamber pot at night instead of using the lavatory down the corridor. Eventually the bedroom steward was so fed up with emptying the pot each morning that while the woman was at breakfast he scoured it clean, filled it with light-ale, and then drank the lot in front of her when she returned. She never used the pot again.

The 'bloods' fascinated me because I saw them so seldom. Like the servant behind the green baize door, I pestered the wingers for details of life upstairs. Mostly they were too busy but the camp waiter known as 'Mary Queen of Scots' gave me renderings of exchanges such as this:

'I say, waiter, there's no card in our cabin,' the fearsome wife of a colonel complained, referring to some notice from the Purser's office.

'Noël Coward in our cabin!' echoed the Colonel. 'What the devil is the fellah doing there?'

After a while a waiter was sent to join me in the fruit locker, which I regarded as my personal territory. An American passenger had asked him what he thought of America. Unwisely, the waiter told him and the American reported the man to the captain, who gave instructions that he should be kept away from the passengers. He took charge of the fruit locker, handing out *my* fruit and juice to his friends while I had to bring them up from the storeroom. He had a wife and child to whom he was devoted and his voyage was one long struggle to save money. I found it curious that so many of the crew were obsessed by their families, yet chose this life of exile. I was delighted when he departed for another, more lucrative job. When the second sitting was over I would hurry on deck for two glorious hours of relaxation, 'bronzing' in the afternoon sun. The days grew hotter as we crossed the Atlantic on our way to Trinidad, though there was always a breeze. We had the forward deck, which I considered the best on the ship, and I leant over the rails watching the ever-changing sea, exulting in the flying fish that skimmed the spray, and the porpoises – or were they dolphins? – which seemed to jump for joy. At such moments I was certain that no other life could be so worthwhile.

Having travelled as crew below decks, I should be afraid to go on a cruise as a passenger, like a stranger in a half-familiar house, listening to laughter from a separate room.

To my surprise I discovered that I was reasonably popular. Although a liner is like a floating hotel in some ways, staff cannot escape at night into a private life of their own. On the *Orcades* there was no privacy, except inside the pages of a book. We were dependent on each other; our relationships concealed nothing, but were impermanent. It could never be the same on land. Friendships were as strange as the individual personalities of the crew. Two of the waiters had sailed together on several voyages. Ten days out they had an argument over a rasher of bacon, which one accused the other of stealing from his plate. Their mutual anger was so deep that they refused to speak to each other, though they continued to sleep in the same cabin and work together. Their silence lasted throughout the voyage. When the ship docked they went their separate ways, never to meet again.

The eight in my cabin seemed an odd lot to me, though no doubt I was even odder. One was a Teddy boy who appeared in full regalia just before we sailed, with a swagger, and smudges of melancholy beneath his eyes. He sat on his bunk for hours, playing with a pocket knife. His double lived in the next cabin and they stuck together, exchanging their few words. Stripped of their tight trousers, velvet collars and 'slim-Jim' ties, they were lost souls.

Owly, the Londoner, moved to another cabin, and was replaced by a peculiar character known as Mad Paddy. It seemed incredible that any doctor could have passed him as fit. He broke most things he touched and when he was on 'stores' he threw a crate so violently that the man next in line refused to work with him. Finally the second steward gave up and Paddy succeeded in doing less than anyone else on board. Tall and stooping, he loped with uncoordinated movements, his endless arms hanging despondently down to his knees. I suspect that he suffered from TB for he was deathly white as if he had crawled out from under a gigantic stone. He was twenty-two and remembered so little of his past that he was not even sure he came from Ireland, and he was the only person I have met whose eyes looked as if they needed dusting.

Paddy had been kicked out of his last cabin because they could stand his smell no longer, and now, in the lowest cabin of all, he could go no further. He had the bunk above me and the smell of his unwashed hair and sockless feet enveloped me. The others threatened to throw him overboard unless he took a shower. Finally they seized him by force and dragged him to the bathroom where he stood miserably in his gum-boots under the unfamiliar water. At the sight of his wormlike body we did not have the heart to go further. Paddy and his smell lingered on; with the shrewdness of the mad, he was a born survivor.

Den was a broad, good-looking young Londoner with a false tooth which he sucked in and out constantly. He was pleasant but dour and needed to be handled with care. At the slightest provocation, he started a fight. Bitterness creased his brow when he told me of his recent prison sentence for robbery with violence. He protested that this had been unjust, but I felt he was lucky not to have been charged with manslaughter.

Bert kept to himself and was disliked by the others. His bunk was under Den's, with whom he had a running battle over the ventilators. A tiresome hypochondriac, he was convinced he was going to catch cold; as soon as it was dark and the air from the ventilators made the hot nights bearable, Bert turned them off. Den would then get out of his bunk, swearing horribly, and turn them on again. Such issues were all-important below decks and we were united against Bert, who did finally catch a chill. He was sent to the hospital for several days and subsequently transferred to another cabin, to our relief.

In the next bunk to mine was 'Marilyn', whose real name was Alfred. He looked far from robust, his pallor heightened by dark, plucked eyebrows. On special occasions he wore black mascara and a scarlet gown which was ripped to shreds later in the voyage. He was small and slim, though not so young as he claimed. Marilyn was unusual in that he had a steady boy-friend and neither made any attempt to conceal the relationship. Moreover, the 'husband' was one of the handsomest waiters on board, a pleasant, smiling man. Beside him, Marilyn looked shrivelled. When I asked about their sex-life Marilyn assured me that 'nothing really happened'. However, another waiter complained to me bitterly of their grunts and groans throughout the night, which could have explained why Marilyn looked so worn out. Marilyn was reviled by the other, envious queens, while the waiter was condemned by his colleagues. The nastier the gossip became, the closer it brought them together.

Looking back, it appears that our cabin attracted freaks, which is not altogether surprising, for the U-gang had no status of its own and was used as a last resort for misfits. Of these, Saint Cecilia was the most bizarre. He joined us after two weeks, having been demoted steadily from his first job as a wine steward. His real name was Cecil and I would have fled from him ordinarily. Large, perspiring and bald, saliva ran weakly from the corner of his mouth, as if there were a leak, and when he spoke it burst out in a verbal spray. Yet he had an endearing enthusiasm. At first he seemed so 'pepped up' that I thought he took drugs, but I saw no evidence of this. In his way, he was indomitable.

Saint Cecilia told me he had been an actor but admitted, 'My dear, it's absolutely finished. No future *there*, which is why I am *here*!' He gave a dreadful guffaw which drenched me in spit. As I was the only person remotely interested in the stage, I was the target for his reminiscences and a stream of theatrical gossip: 'Dear Celia, my namesake, now there's a lovely actress . . .' 'What wicked things the press are saying about John' and 'I always say that Noël is a real professional.'

Naïvely, I was much impressed by his references to the stars and to the productions he had been in at Drury Lane or the Haymarket, until I discovered that his role was that of scene-shifter. The closest he came to treading the boards was in a Northern panto-mime as a hump-backed footman.

These were my cabin mates.

At first I was so tired at the end of the day that all I wished for was sleep. Later, when I had cleaned and locked the fruit locker after the last sitting, I hurried to the cabin to change out of my dripping T-shirt and join the line on deck, mug in hand, for the weak beer which was the only drink we could buy from the Pig and Whistle. Even then, there was seldom time for more than a pint or two. Afterwards we would sit on deck, watching the stewards dance with each other or with other exhibitionists among the crew, to rock and roll on the gramophone. If the weather was bad we went down to the rec-room, which sported an old piano, useful for the occasional drag-show, and prints of Renoir and Van Gogh, which looked singularly ill at ease in such surroundings. There were other distractions: wrestling bouts and a film show once a week on the crew deck.

As we sailed into the sun I appreciated my kingdom of the fruit locker, with its port-hole, ice-chest and supplies of fruit juice. I took as many cold showers as possible, but even so, I soon began to suffer from prickly heat. When the cabin became too stifling, I slept a couple of nights on deck under a blanket of stars. It was uncomfortable and the dawn far from romantic.

After a week we sighted the green hills of Trinidad, their peaks darkened by the over-hanging cloud. We anchored three miles out from Port of Spain. The passengers were ferried ashore, but we were confined on board because the last crew had returned late and fighting drunk thanks to cheap local rum.

To compensate, I was determined to go ashore at Panama, but I was broke. Fortu-nately the assistant second admired a pair of moccasins my father had given me and bought them for two dollars. There was only one sitting for dinner and I shared the im-patience of the waiters as the bloods dallied interminably over their meal. At last I got my shore-pass and ran down the gangway at Bilbao. Ten of us crowded into a taxi and headed for Panama City, a honky-tonk town of such immodest charm that I was not sur-prised my father had once spent the night there in the local 'cooler'.

I relished every second of my brief taste of Panama, which lasted little more than an hour. There was one main street with a row of bars, deafening music, patrols of American Military Police, and some of the loveliest women I have seen. The street parodied the set of an American musical; off it, I plunged into sudden darkness which gradually revealed wooden houses, their front rooms open like a sideshow, with people eating, sewing or swaying gently on their rocking chairs.

Time was precious both on board and on land. I was shocked to think of the hours I had wasted in Soho, of mornings when I stayed in bed after nine o'clock; now I yearned for just one afternoon of undiluted leisure. I appreciated the value of money, too. My first wage-packet was a shock. Instead of the ten pounds I expected, I received three, due to the deduction of income-tax, two pounds retained in case of fines, union dues and the cost of regulation kit. Three pounds for two weeks, with America ahead.

Our first stop was a drowsy resort: Long Beach, self-styled as the 'Queen of the Beaches'. We lined up at 5.30 a.m. to fill in the absurdly detailed immigration forms and receive our passes. We coincided with a 'killer heatwave' – sixty people had sizzled to death in nearby Los Angeles. A police-car gave me a lift into town.

'It was 108 yesterday,' said the cop laconically, 'hottest we've ever known.' I was already sunburnt and looked at the sea longingly.

'Are there sharks?' I asked.

'Not in the water,' he replied with a smile, 'on shore, plenty.'

He dropped me outside a drugstore, refreshingly cool with a juke-box playing soft music and an inexplicable range of goods – from vodka to stuffed pandas, beauty-aids and paperbacks advising me How to Make More Money, Eat and Get Slim, and Be Glad You're Neurotic. I returned to the sweltering sun outside. Have Your Blood Tested, snapped a neon sign; Lose that Fat, urged a photograph of a large lady. The bodies of the skimpily clad passers-by belied this emphasis on health.

The endless amusement park sported a flea circus, an Ossified Man, and The World's Greatest Ride, but it was all too hygienic for me, lacking the shabby thrill of Panama.

San Francisco was elating by comparison. When we entered the bay a morning mist hung over the Golden Gate, which is really red. The mist cleared suddenly and the other great span of the graceful Oakland Bay Bridge shimmered in the sunlight as we passed the grim island of Alcatraz. The city before us sloped up the hill, as radiant as if it had just been washed. Most arrivals in port have excitement, and this is one of the best. I hung over the rail, enchanted as the *Orcades* docked slowly in the centre of the waterfront.

My luck was in. The mail delivered on board included a cheque for six pounds from *Harper's* magazine for the reproduction of a small photograph. Half had to be saved for Vancouver and beyond, but the cheque was made out in dollars so it was easy to cash. Astonishing good fortune! I was rich indeed, for few cities are so welcoming as San Francisco as it was in simpler days.

As I walked up the hill in the late afternoon the city had a curiously deserted, lethargic air, which was appealing. The Teddy boy walked beside me wearing his velvet collar, his hair carefully coiffed into a DA. 'They look at us as if we're from Mars,' he complained.

Teddy and I moved on to Chinatown which turned out to be as sedate as a side-street in Hove, scattered with souvenir shops, and we parted company in the Barbara Coast, for Teddy was looking for a strip-club while I wanted to wander. There are some nights when everything goes your way, and this proved one of them.

Before I sailed, I had shopped at Vince, started by Bill Green, the unacknowledged founder of Carnaby Street, who brought a new sense of fun to clothes in that gloomy post-war period, when it was hard to be young. The peacockiness of the Teddy-boys was frowned on, but Vince specialised in narrow, tight blue-jeans and light, canvas zip-up jackets long before they became fashionable. The clothes made me conspicuous. Stumbling on the Black Carnation, a smoky, crowded bar in a vast cellar, my Vince gear and now bronzed face singled me out as a British Merchant Seaman. I was instantly popular; it was a good feeling.

People were dancing, the atmosphere was boisterous, and when the club closed I was driven to a warehouse which sold illicit drink. In the loft above more young people danced to an old jangle-box piano by candlelight until four in the morning when ten of us moved on to one of the old houses which survived the earthquake. At the top was a penthouse that was more like a greenhouse. The glass roof was so high that it enclosed trees as well as shrubs. A butler brought trays of glasses and drinks and one of the young men acted as if he knew the place well. When the butler asked me if I would be so kind as to follow him, the young man gave me a nod, and murmured, 'Please.' I followed the servant through the jungle to a bedroom where a distinguished old man lay in bed, wide awake. The butler withdrew and the old man waved me towards the bed with an attempt at a smile.

'How kind of you to come to see me. Your first visit.' He spoke with such exquisite politeness that the next sentence jarred: 'And you're English, in the Merch?' In the clipped tones of Clifton Webb he then asked me to remove my 'pants'. I gaped. 'Nothing more,' he added reassuringly. Feeling it would be churlish to refuse, I started to undo my jeans, but he waved a hand impatiently: 'Don't *drop* them, take them off.' Too startled to argue, I undid my baseball boots and took off my jeans. 'Ah,' said the old man appreciatively. I stood there in a pair of Vince's very brief briefs, needing a peaked leather cap and a motor bike to complete the parody of a model in a physique magazine.

That was all; he sank back on the pillows with a weary smile and the butler reappeared, handing me an envelope, which I opened behind an orange tree. It contained ten dollars.

On to Vancouver and the invigorating approach of red earth, forests and snow peaks above the clouds. The air was crisp and cool and scented with pine, but the town suffered from that dismaying Canadian gentility. The bars looked wild and brassy from the outside, as giants from the outback staggered in with fistfuls of money, only to sit down at small tables, with a Palm Court orchestra playing sedately in the background. Occasionally the formality would be shattered by a lumberjack rising to smash a chair over another man's head.

In the Pacific the ever-changing skies were vaster and more magnificent than ever. The *Orcades* had taken on more passengers for the trip to Sydney, fruit-obsessed Americans who demanded such quantities that my locker was besieged by wingers shouting their orders like revolutionaries. The pressure was such that I was given an assistant, Walter. A bellboy with the ageless face of a Stan Laurel, he told me of his home with macabre pride: 'You know the sawn-off-shot-gun murder case?'

'I think so.'

'Well, you know the man shot himself after killing the woman?'

'Yes.' (I found it saved time to say 'yes'.)

'And the policeman who found the body?'

'Yes.'

'Well, he lives at the end of our street.'

When I asked if he had enjoyed his trip ashore in Frisco he beamed with pleasure: 'I went for a drive with some people, and they showed me that cliff where all those people were killed. I had a smashing time, me.'

The increase in passengers put the chief steward in a bad temper and he patrolled the galley more frequently, jeopardising my meals. I worked out a warning signal with Walter. He would stand outside the locker whilst I was shelling Pacific prawns and burst into song when someone approached. A meant the chief; B the second. 'A – you're adorable,' he warbled in a ghastly cracked voice, and I swallowed hard before the chief ambled in, sweeping his fishy eyes over me. Or 'Bee-cause you're mine!' It kept Walter occupied.

I made particular friends with a winger called Sam. We used to meet on deck because he refused to go to the Pig and Whistle or the rec-room.

'It's my gesture against the ship,' he explained. 'I don't want any part of the life.'

'A pretty silly gesture,' I pointed out. 'I don't suppose anyone notices if you come to the Pig or not.'

He slapped his leg in irritation. 'Don't you *see*? I'm trying to make my life as unpleasant as possible. Every time I'm home I swear it's for good, but after a couple of weeks I'm broke and sign on again. Now I've given up smoking. I want to hate the life on board so much that nothing will bring me back after this trip.' A seaman who hated the sea, he suffered from a discontent worthy of Lord Jim.

Sam was a romantic, yearning for higher things, anxious to learn. The discovery that I read books brought us together; he was a loner otherwise.

At Honolulu Teddy showed me a press cutting which had just arrived in the ship's mail – his girl-friend had been sent to a remand home, though she looked harmless in the photograph. 'I'm shocked,' the magistrate was reported as saying, 'to hear of girls like you going around with horrid little Teddy boys.'

Teddy was baffled and deeply hurt. 'Me?' He frowned. 'A horrid little Teddy? What's 'e on about?'

Wakiki Beach proved beyond the imagining, unspoilt except for stalls selling hamburgers and cool root beer after our swim. In the evening three of us decided to get tattooed. The ship was about to sail and we were broke, so the tattoo had to be quick and small. After looking at the dozens of designs we settled on a small fish. Francis Bacon later referred to it as a sardine; it was meant to be a shark. Some impulse persuaded us to have the 'shark' tattooed on the left hand, a painful place because of the lack of flesh. I found it agonising, but was proud when it was finished and a piece of lavatory paper was placed on top to help it heal. My pride was shattered by the reaction on board: 'Marked for life,' spluttered Saint Cecilia gleefully. 'You'll regret it, just you see. Hah! As long as you live.'

Someone added that people with tattoos were especially prone to epilepsy, and I began to notice the other tattoos on board. Some were extraordinary in their complexity

– crucifixion scenes on the chest, shipwrecks on the back, tombstones on the arms, and plenty of names 'In Memory'. An aged night-watchman had had the head of Queen Victoria tattooed on him when he was a boy Marine in Portsmouth at the turn of the century. Another had E M P T Y in large letters across his stomach, and there were the familiar L O V E and H A T E on the fingers of either hand, which struck me as sad. Geisha girls tattooed in the Far East were the most beautiful, small works of art in their own eccentric way.

After Hawaii we sailed for a week before we reached Suva, the capital of Fiji. The *Orcades* had the Governor on board and after passing through the coral reefs we drew alongside an open square where gigantic policemen in scarlet tunics and ragged white skirts lined up to be inspected. A band struck up as the Governor stepped ashore, saluting smartly. The scene resembled a 'primitive' painting with the green hills behind, and the air was redolent with coconut oil.

On shore, several of us clambered over a wall into a swimming pool, ignoring the agitated cries of a caretaker until we caught the word 'typhus' and realised why the pool was closed. The next day we shared a taxi and crossed those green hills scattered with villages. We swam naked in the open sea, off sand fringed by thick green forest without a building in sight.

Finally we approached Australia. For days conversation below decks centred on the tips expected from the passengers – dropsy from the bloods.

This was the purpose of the voyage and the atmosphere was tense. The wingers had schemed for this moment. If a passenger asked for an order which wasn't on the menu, though perfectly easy to get, they made it sound so difficult that when they appeared with the dish it seemed a triumph. All except Sam. On principle he treated his bloods so casually that there was no question of tips, and to make doubly sure he stayed in the plate-house after the last sitting so that he would not be there to receive them. Ironically, his passengers adored him and I heard they had even prepared a little speech. Instead, they filled an envelope with pound notes, which made him deeply depressed, a hostage to the sea once more.

There was very nearly a riot in the saloons the night before we docked. The Greek wingers abused certain passengers for their meanness and even fought them. At first, with my wretched streak of priggishness, I was shocked. Then I learnt of the passengers' behaviour and was even more shocked. After a voyage of two months one passenger gave a tip of ten shillings. The winger called over one of the bellboys and gave it to him instead. When another was offered five shillings, the winger gave it back contemptuously.

'Obviously you need this more than I do,' he said.

'Perhaps so,' snapped the passenger, still discomfited by the sight of his winger, who was one of the sharply dressed 'cowboys' sitting at the next table in the Honolulu night club where he had taken his family.

One woman left three 2 ½d. stamps under a plate, but she was forgiven because she was old. Others gave as little as 2s. 6d., and some sneaked away without paying at all. I saw one Greek waiter in tears, and another had to be forcibly restrained by the second steward (who revealed remarkable sympathy in the circumstances) to prevent him from fighting an Australian who left nothing while insisting on another helping of ice-cream. Conversely, other wingers came back through the swing-doors as satisfied as cream-swilling cats to count their rewards of up to forty pounds. The Americans were the most generous.

As a small flea, I hoped for tips from the wingers to whom I had given special service. I placed a box with a few coins on the edge of the locker and gave some to Teddy to drop in noisily as he raced by with his tray. Teddy forgot and somehow I ended the sitting five shillings short. I was recompensed later, albeit disastrously, as I shall relate.

All was tranquil in the morning when we sailed into Sydney Harbour. I hurried on deck at 5.00 a.m. to watch our arrival and heard American voices above me.

'What a cute château,' said one woman.

'My, that Captain Cook must have been real captivated!' exclaimed another.

I was less captivated, too rigid in my expectations. One of the finest natural harbours in the world, a jig-saw of small bays and inlets, Sydney was the perfect site for imaginative building, yet I felt the opportunity had been ignored. Like most Englishmen, I was annoyed by things being similar yet subtly different. The taxis were peculiarly convivial. In the first a large lady sat beside the driver playing cards. I think she was the largest woman I have seen.

'I can see yer a sport,' she greeted me in a beery voice. 'How many cabs will we see before we get there? I'll bet-ya.'

I said I hadn't the faintest idea.

'Aw, go on,' she persisted.

'All right, twenty-five,' I guessed submissively.

'Good on yer,' she exclaimed, 'and a dollar for me if it's over.'

As we drove on she counted triumphantly and I paid up grudgingly after the taxi had stopped several times to pick up other passengers and veered off in different directions.

Surprisingly, I was even disappointed by Bondi Beach, finding it small and suburban. So much for the treachery of first impressions, aggravated by the dreary weather, the general air of despondency, lack of money, or by the fact that the area at Pyrmont where we landed was desolate and grey. Yet at Pyrmont I found the Montgomery and I needed to look no further for good times. Monty's was a great dockland pub with a happy confusion of people and it was here, on our second night in port, that I made friends with a group of Australian dockers. They drove three of us to a ramshackle wooden house in Paddington, which they kept as a hideaway for all-night parties. The last of these, before we sailed, should have been the best, yet turned sour. There were new faces, arguments, and I lost my Vince canvas jacket. Many of the crew were glum for reasons of their own: some had been beaten up, with cuts and bruises to prove it. Two bedroom stewards had dragged two strangers back to their cabin and woke to find that all their rings and jewellery had gone. They received scant sympathy. Saint Cecilia had been arrested, so the rumour went; certainly he had disappeared after the first night, when he had been seen on another ship that had docked at the same time, visiting the cabins as if he were taking an inventory, gossiping as he criticised. He was picked up the next night climbing over the wall of a public lavatory. Probably the Australian police were thankful to get rid of him. He was fined and sent back to the gangway. He had two black eyes but remained defiant: 'Wee! I told that judge. "You want bloody immigrants, do you? Then you must be mad. This place is a bloody *disgrace*."' He seemed rather shaken all the same.

There was violence on board as well. The brother of Marilyn's 'husband' happened to be on the other ship too. In Monty's he was told about his brother's infatuation by a jealous bedroom steward and arrived on the *Orcades* to find his brother in his cabin, with Marilyn sitting on his knee, wearing the scarlet party dress. The two brothers fought each other silently until they no longer had the heart to do so. The waiter turned on Marilyn when his brother left, tore the dress to pieces and never spoke to Marilyn again. I saw the two brothers together in Monty's the next day talking and laughing as if nothing had happened.

'I *hate* this place,' said Marilyn with sudden intensity as we looked down at the quayside before we sailed. 'There's always trouble.'

We stared at the crowds below who had come to say goodbye to relatives and friends. I was always moved by this moment of departure: the brightness of the band seemed so inappropriate; small boys scrambled for cigarettes and money thrown down by the passengers and even the crew; coloured streamers flew with mock gaiety and people shouted awkwardly as they waited interminably for the ship to move, filled with sudden panic when she did so. A girl cried out, 'I love you, I love you!' as if she had not been sure until this moment, and an old woman shook with grief that was inconsolable because she knew this was the final farewell.

The first time I saw Auckland it was wet and dismal and I drank the worst cup of coffee I had ever tasted. The next day it was glorious sunshine. I climbed to the top of Mount Eden, an extinct volcano, and looked over the town and the countryside for miles around, with green islands in the distance and not an ugly building in sight. I walked back to the docks through pleasant residential streets, stopping at a bar where people asked me what part of 'home' I had come from.

The second bar was my undoing. This was filled with crew from the *Orcades* drinking against the curfew – the infamous 'five o'clock swill' was about to begin. In those days the pubs closed at six and this final hour was additionally desperate because the ship was about to sail. Plastic pipes poured beer into our schooner glasses with the speed of an alcoholic garage, and it was now that the wingers repaid me for my services by ordering me drinks while refusing to let me buy any in return. The rounds whirled so swiftly that half-a-dozen glasses of whisky were thrust before me at a time. Whisky has never been my favourite drink since my first appalled taste of it at Cambridge, yet I could hardly refuse. The alcohol took effect suddenly. While wiser members of the crew collapsed into a cab, I burst out of the bar and charged down the main street with the *Orcades* waiting forbiddingly at the bottom of the hill.

Other members of the crew stumbled with me and we were joined by two passengers who were part of a circus troupe: a midget, and his close friend 'the largest man in the world', who had played Goliath in a film. A gaping crowd of children who had never witnessed such a sight ran after us, and I remember little else.

I came to with a splitting headache in my bunk, fully clothed, with Saint Cecilia spluttering over me, which did not make me feel better. 'You're for it!' he chuckled. 'It's the bridge for you. Better look out!' He told me that while I was unconscious the second steward had entered the cabin, looked down at me, and said with a smile, 'I'm going to squeeze that dish-cloth dry.' Saint Cecilia was understandably confused: 'What did he mean?'

I groaned, knowing all too well. I had posted an article to the *Evening Standard* about joining the Merchant Navy, which was published under the heading 'Around the World with a Dish-cloth'. Plainly, this had reached the upper deck.

Several of us assembled outside the bridge, most with aching hangovers, which gave us a conspiratorial kinship. I wore my pristine uniform. One man warned me that the captain was in a vile mood after a cabin inspection, when he had torn down calendars and photographs of girls exclaiming, 'Filthy! You must be sex-maniacs!' His temper was so uncontrollable that officers on his last ship had mutinied. 'So you'd better look out,' said the man.

'*Farson*! Inside.'

I was marched into a room where the captain sat at a table in the middle of a line of officers, the Union Jack behind him. When he addressed me, he was scarcely able to control himself.

'Around the world with a sweatrag. I suppose you think that's funny, but we don't like people who write about what we do aboard.' I tried to look expressionless though his venom astounded me.

'You're here to do a job,' he shrilled, 'not write for the cheap London press.'

For a moment I thought I was going to laugh, but I managed to stop myself and prepared myself for the next indictment. I knew the captain had a phobia about seamen dodging National Service, but he could hardly accuse me of that. For a moment he paused, then, with a splutter worthy of Saint Cecilia, he cried: 'You've come to sea to dodge something. What is it? I know . . .' He leant forward menacingly. 'You've come to sea to dodge taking photographs.'

This time it was harder not to laugh, but I kept quiet. Disappointed, he sat back and concluded: '103 each charge, half a day's forfeiture and if you're up on the bridge again, a bad discharge.'

I heard afterwards that he believed I had collapsed on purpose in order to write about my experience on the bridge, but I have never needed an excuse to drink.

The incident enhanced my reputation considerably with the crew. Suddenly we were homeward bound. Colombo in Ceylon, the most beautiful coastline of all; Bombay;

Aden, which looked mysterious and raffish; the Suez Canal; Marseilles. The cold in the English channel penetrated our bones and I realised how thin my blood had become. On the infamous Channel night, when old scores were settled, Marilyn was beaten up by a stoker and Saint Cecilia tried, ineffectually, to kill himself.

The moment we docked at Tilbury it was all forgotten. I regretted bitterly giving Saint Cecilia my address, for the thought of him 'dropping in' was suddenly appalling. I shivered in the freezing, unfamiliar cold as I hurried down the gangway and ran for the train to Liverpool street.

In Soho I went into the French pub where instead of a barrage of questions I was absorbed into the old, familiar conversation. I might not have been away.

The Fleet's In

When I arrived in Antalya in October 1988, the US fleet was moored outside. It looked as if it had never gone away, for the *Eisenhower*, a massive aircraft carrier, had straddled the sea on my first visit in May. Now the *John F. Kennedy* marked another presidential visit. If the *Orcades* was a floating hotel, the *Kennedy* was a floating city.

The old harbour was filled with a carnival spirit as the Turks waited for the American sailors to land. The harbour has been restored so successfully, with bars and restaurants on different levels, and a fountain with ducks, which delight the Turkish children, that the scene is always popular, but when the fleet comes in it's riotous.

Inevitably, the touts descend but they are good-humoured, having learnt the art of patience. There is none of the 'baksheesh' harassment which pursues you through the rest of the Middle East. The bargaining is a serious game, conducted with surprising courtesy on either side. A group of sailors in civilian clothes, young men wistfully anxious to like and to be liked, step from their liberty-boats on to Turkish soil. They are accosted by grinning Turks who hold up rugs of fascinating vulgarity depicting a group of cigar-smoking bulldogs playing pool; a simpering Madonna; a lion slouched in a conventional though hideous sitting-room; and numerous American eagles and Stars and Stripes flags, adorned with skulls and motor-bikes. Do the sailors believe these are genuine Turkish carpets?

One sailor looked on indifferently as horror after horror was flung in obeisance before him. Finally, after lengthy bargaining he yielded to a black panther snarling on the branch of a tree, and both sides shook hands, each believing himself the winner.

These young men seemed so decent, so innocent, so well-mannered. The *Kennedy* holds 5,000 men so they have to live together harmoniously or life would be insufferable, but as we talked I sensed the undercurrents which exist below this placid surface. Officially there is no colour prejudice and I saw numerous black and white sailors walking in pairs, laughing amiably, but racism runs deep: 'I hate them and their goddamn rap music,' one white sailor said.

I wondered what they made of me, no longer a participant but a curious observer in every sense. When I explained that I was once a GI myself, they listened politely but I doubted if they believed a word of it. It seemed so unlikely. Learning that I write books, a clean-cut, well-scrubbed young officer alerted the others: 'Hey, this man has written a *book*! I'd like to shake your hand, sir. I've read a book or two, but jeez, never thought I'd meet someone who's written one.'

Over the next few evenings, I got to know a group who used the bar in my hotel and looked uneasy in the marbled opulence. A large unkempt sailor invited me to go with them: 'Will you join us, Mr Daniel, sir? You seem like a good old boy.' They said that about President Carter's brother, Billy, but I was deeply flattered and agreed.

Ron was thirty-six, amiability personified. As a boiler technician he was in charge of several men who regarded him with obvious respect in spite of his macho *badinage* and playful wrestling. He guarded the younger men as they grew increasingly drunk. In a way that was wholly innocent, you could sense that he loved them.

One man stood apart because of his lean physical strength, a natural 'roughneck', except that his clear blue eyes told of a deep regret. I suspected that his temper was short and was proved correct. Al had been court-martialled a few years earlier for beating up a man to the point of death. 'There was cause,' he shrugged, his voice low and his pock-marked face expressionless, 'but I could have been Ron's supervisor now instead of the other way around.'

'Are you bitter?'

'It rankles. Ron's fair, you couldn't get fairer than Ron. After my court-martial I left the Navy and worked as a guard in a prison – I needed to punish myself and this was the worst job I could think of. It taught me. Seeing some of the characters there taught me to control my temper. I thought, no way am I going to end up like them, so I re-enlisted.'

With the intimacy between strangers who will never meet again, he produced his wallet, removing photographs of his family – two boys wrestling and a smiling young woman. Though Al will retire at thirty-eight, he'll have missed the tenderest years.

Another of the sailors worked on the flight deck. 'Wouldn't work anywhere else in spite of the danger,' he said. Jet-waves had made Eric colour blind and his fingers were bandaged because a pilot had closed his cockpit on them accidentally. 'Still, I consider myself lucky, so far. If anything's caught by the jet less than fifteen feet away, it's sucked in and the whole engine has to be dismantled.'

'You don't mean *you* could be sucked in?'

'Sure. Last trip one little fellow disappeared that way.'

'Christ!' I exclaimed. 'With human flesh, hair, teeth and bones, that must be messy a business.'

Eric gave a knowing smile. 'Naw! Not a bit of it. If you're sucked in, you come out like *talc*!'

A Stranger in England

I doubt if I would have explored the north of England, and certainly not the mundane Midlands, without the spur of the television series *Members' Mail* (the curious title referred to correspondence sent to an MP by his constituents) and, particularly, my series of documentaries, *Farson's Guide to the British*.

My explorations convinced me that parts of Britain were every bit as strange as 'abroad'. The diversity and the glorious eccentricity of the British delighted me; in a single back street in a northern town I found more life than in the whole of Ottawa. Northerners have qualities lacking in the south, where there is more money and time for pretension. Southerners wait to be entertained; northerners seize their fun. They are not ashamed to show their emotions – I remember seeing pensioners dancing merrily in a sporting club and when the group started to play 'We've Been Together Now for Forty Years', the old couples at the long table near me linked hands, kissed each other affectionately and sang the familiar words with tears running down their cheeks.

Hospitality is spontaneous. Hearing I had nowhere to sleep one night, a working man in a pub in Barrow-in-Furness insisted that I return to his home, and though the small house was swollen with dogs and children, his wife welcomed me as if she was expecting my arrival.

I warmed to the cities of the north. The great black banks in Manchester might have been carved from coal in rich satanic canyons, and I was startled to see the prow of a ship beyond some rubble, unaware that Manchester is our third busiest port, with miles of canal bringing water from the sea.

Take a train from Manchester to Liverpool, barely half an hour away, and it is as if you

have crossed a frontier: people look different, speak differently, with a jaunty sense of humour. In the late 1950s the centre of Liverpool resembled ancient Rome, but the interminable docks were stark with poverty, which explained why the young were thankful to escape into the Merchant Navy or made their own music, inspired by sea shanties and folk songs, West Indian and Chinese influences, and the latest American beat brought back in the big ships from America – a colourful fusion bound together by the raw exuberance of Liverpool itself.

Tea on the Lawn at Cheltenham

Cheltenham conjured up a backwater of dear old ladies and retired colonels, good for a laugh in musical comedies, along with Scunthorpe and Chorlton-cum-Hardy.

The façade confirmed the reputation: a leafy promenade with balustrades and graceful Georgian houses, and the rotunda at the end upheld by the decorative figures of slaves: 'It wasn't the thing for servants to walk there when we called it Calcutta Country,' I was told. The town grew from the spa, which was built in 1783 and visited fifty years later by George III, who rose at six to take his exercise by walking round the town after drinking several glasses of the spa water. When I visited, the waters were sold in the Town Hall. Since they were supposed to provide a miraculous cure for hangovers, I followed suit and recovered instantly, unlike the unfortunate woman whose experience was lamented in verse:

> Here lie I and my two daughters,
> Died through drinking Cheltenham waters.
> If we'd but stuck to Epsom salts
> We'd not be lying in these vaults.

Behind the façade, a different character lurked. I was told that the town 'enjoyed' one of the highest illegitimacy rates in the country, which suggested that the colonels were still on active service, and I admired their fortitude when I was assured that 'It only happens *in* closed doors.'

I found the essence of Cheltenham one lazy afternoon when I had tea with the Misses Fawkes, three sisters in their eighties. Their house was proof of their activities: flower arrangements, embroidery, music, painting – the admirable skills encouraged in gentle-women of their time. We had tea from a large silver teapot, accompanied by home-made fruit-cake and thin sandwiches, sitting on a well-kept lawn with a mulberry tree and bees buzzing in the herbaceous borders.

It became obvious that the Misses Fawkes did not know a moment of boredom.

'Archery,' was the surprising answer when I asked one of the sisters about her favourite pastime in the town.

'I like crime,' replied another. 'My sister likes historical novels.'

'We've seen the television once,' said the first, 'to watch the Gold Cup Race. We're waiting for the coloured television before we have a set, so much more interesting then, don't you think?'

If other interests dared to fail them, there was always their passion: the garden. It was a drowsy, shimmering summer's day and as I talked to the Misses Fawkes my attention was caught by a figure in mauve among the trees. No sooner had I caught sight of it than it would disappear, like the 'ghosts' seen by the two English women at Versailles. My apparition came to life when Mrs Fisher appeared on the lawn. I saw that she was carrying a small stool which she unfolded whenever she found a particularly favourable place to examine the flowers, and hence disappeared from view.

Mrs Fisher had known grander days. Now she stayed in a nursing home nearby and the Misses Fawkes gave her the freedom of their garden, where she spent fine afternoons. Mrs Fisher was not a 'dear old lady'; she was a radiant, deeply humorous woman, with a resonant delivery and pauses which were so compelling that I assumed she had been on the stage. She was eighty-nine and still beautiful. I commented that old people in Cheltenham seemed exceptionally lively.

'Old people nowadays,' she confirmed, 'when they get past . . . what shall we say? . . . (a long pause) sixty or seventy, they take on a new lease of life and there's no holding them. They may go on for goodness knows how long . . . *for ever*!'

We talked about her travels and all the places she had visited – Paris, the Riviera, New Zealand. 'Is Cheltenham the most beautiful?' I asked which prompted the vigorous response: 'Oh *no*! If you really want to know, the most beautiful city in Europe was Budapest, and then Paris. When I come back on earth, my itinerary – as the Americans say – will be Paris for fun and laughter. And then I'm going to Italy, to be quite serious with Michelangelo.'

'What has been your happiest moment?'

'Dancing on the Riviera – *lately*!'

'And what is the greatest disappointment of old age?'

'When you don't get a nice lunch.'

The Gusto of the Age

Other countries have them too, but there is something particularly gallant about the British seaside resort, in defiance of the elements. In more innocent times they were described as 'the gusto of the age', combining the happy vulgarity of music hall with the wistful yearning for new horizons.

There was nothing modest about the seaside resort and that was part of the allure. It began when a gentlewoman visited Scarborough as far back as 1626, drank the spring water and found it so revolting that she announced it must be health-giving. Gradually the town became fashionable as 'the Queen of English Watering Places', when the gentry decided that a breath of sea-air, and even a swallow of salt water, did them good. The Scarborough resort was conceived on a grand scale, with hotels like palaces, a Gothic saloon and concert hall, designed by the finest architects of the day. The transition from spa to resort was confirmed in 1846 when the railways brought thousands of workers from the industrial centres inland eager to escape 'the smell of oil and the clank of the steam hammer'. Arriving like cattle in open trains, they were made as welcome as the gentry in their carriages with yellow wheels and silver fittings. Even the station was decorated in a style known as 'Luxemburg late-renaissance' and when the English climate sank to the occasion, as it invariably does, the visitors went to the People's Palace, which offered grottoes and models of the Niagara Falls and New York, or to the Aquarium, the Oriental Theatre, the Arcadian Fun Palace or the Floral Hall. When the sun penetrated the sands below the curving esplanade, so did the holiday-makers and the donkeys, the Punch and Judy Shows, and the white-clad Pierrots in ruffles and pointed caps. Cheerful children and excited dogs ran everywhere.

An oyster stall among the crowds on the beach at Blackpool.

That first sight of the sea was a memorable moment in childhood. It did not matter if it was cold or raining, it was *different*. You knew that even before you saw the ocean, its presence announced by the seagulls and the smell of salt.

A man who was brought up in Manchester described his first visit to Blackpool in 1950 when he was ten years old. He stayed in a sort of holiday-concentration-camp where supervisors patrolled the dormitory at night with leather straps to quell the high spirits. Armed with pocket money of 4s. 6d. he had the extraordinary luck of finding half-a-crown on the beach, which he lavished on 'treats' – the fun fair on Pleasure Beach and a surfeit of burgers and fried onions.

Blackpool offered different styles of entertainment. You had it 'posh', with oysters at the bar, and you had it rude, with side-shows on the Golden Mile – clowns and custard-pies and elephants. Crowded pubs had lady pianists with lacquered hair-dos as erect

as candy floss, and sequined ladies twirled together in the Tower ballroom to the blare of the White Wurlitzer organ.

Coarse comedians, such as Frank Randle, filled the theatres. The idol of the north and the 'uncrowned king of Blackpool', his brand of humour failed to travel south. His dreadful behaviour and drunkenness – 'Baaa, I've supped some ale toneet!' was a catch phrase – dismayed the local councillors who felt they had to express their appreciation of his extraordinary popularity which filled Blackpool during Wakes Week when the mills closed down and towns like Oldham emptied. A dinner was out of the question, because he'd be too inebriated, so they settled on a civic lunch. He surprised them by arriving in his chauffeur-driven limousine, on time, with his teeth in, and cold sober. After a few introductory remarks, Randle announced that he was honoured by the luncheon attended by so many dignitaries and invited the mayor to let the banquet commence. With a sigh of relief, Mr Mayor started to lead the way, pausing to introduce the lady beside him: 'Mr Randle, this is the wife.'

Randle gave her a withering look and returned to form: 'Well, that's your fooking hard luck!'

'If you try to resist the carnival atmosphere, you'll hate it here,' one of the formidable Blackpool landladies told me. 'You've got to have a sense of humour to come here, it's as much a part of Blackpool as the reek of fried food.' Her reputation as a dragon tended to crack when her guests said goodbye: 'Tears are shed openly then, even by me. Everybody gets a splash!'

When the illuminations along the Golden Mile are switched on at the start of the season, it is still a big occasion. The landladies are the most dreaded audiences at the previews of the summer shows, for it is their recommendation that fills the theatres. At the end of the season, the landladies usually present a show of their own, dancing a riotous can-can before they fly off to Tenerife for a well-earned rest.

Entertainment is crucial to the seaside resort, ranging from the old-fashioned concert party to 'olde tyme' music hall. George Melly, who is an admirer of northern comedians, the seedier the better, was enchanted by a comic in one of the smaller Blackpool theatres: a pedantic, unsmiling man with specs, who fantasised that one of the stalwart women in the front row, wearing a floral printed dress, was none other than the Duchess of Kent. Solemnly announcing that they had been honoured by the presence of royalty, he interspersed his appalling jokes – 'I call it suppository furniture because you put it up yourself' – with unctuous bows and references to the startled lady, who watched him open-mouthed throughout.

In contrast to the lavish spectaculars at the Winter Garden, the Fun House on Pleasure Beach is more like a fairground. A massive clown laughs raucously in a glass case outside, beneath a sign that reads 'The second greatest European attraction after the Vatican'.

Southern resorts were always more demure. Only the 'best people' (and how on earth do you define them?) went to Sidmouth, while Teignmouth once held formal Flannel Dances in the afternoon, so named because of the young men who lined one side of the ballroom dressed in grey flannel bags and blazers. There was no bar, no trouble, and dancing stopped at midnight. The climax of the week was walking the girl you fancied home after the last waltz on Saturday evenings.

On the pier at Teignmouth there were Pierrots who sang Patriotic Songs, while a one-legged man jumped off the side in flames. Paddle steamers ferried passengers between the major resorts, until the steam train transformed distant fishing villages like Newquay into fashionable towns. The gentry stayed in smart new hotels with appropriate names such as The Great Western, while their servants were shunted into smaller, rented cottages nearby.

When the station was opened in Torquay, the town declared a public holiday. With its palm trees and kinder climate, Torquay cultivated its image as a sub-tropical paradise to encourage upper-class visitors.

Railways were essential in establishing a resort, even in the case of Brighton, blessed with the royal patronage of Prinny. As many as 73,000 passengers arrived by train in a single week in 1859. Only eleven resorts were listed officially in 1848, compared to hundreds at the end of the century. They included Scarborough and Brighton, of course, Margate, Worthing, Hyde, Dover, Cowes, Torquay and Ilfracombe. Ilfracombe is the odd one out for the railway reached there as late as 1874. The explanation is simple: steam ships came from Cardiff and Swansea across the Bristol Channel. If you visit the museum below the Tropical Gardens, the early prints and photographs show how it was transformed from a fishing village with a single street into an elegant Victorian resort. An arcade was lined with high-class shops; arches of ferns and flowers were erected to celebrate royal occasions. Bathing was prim, and the tunnels built in 1836 remain. Donkeys pulled the bathing huts on iron wheels to the edge of the sea 'to spare the ladies immodesty and deprive the gentlemen of a moment's titillation'. An old lady in her eighties told me she could not remember a woman walking across the beach: 'In fact I do not think she would have been allowed to do it!' A bugler perched on the rocks separating the sexes, ready to sound a warning blast if he saw a gentleman trying to sneak up unawares.

Like Torquay, Ilfracombe was snobbish. When the Ilfracombe Hotel opened in 1861, with 250 bedrooms and charging four guineas a week, it was said that you needed a title to stay there. The Kaiser did so as a boy. This was Ilfracombe's heyday. After the Second World War, the Pavilion was torn down; the wrought-iron bandstand sold for scrap; and the Ilfracombe Hotel, renamed the Holiday Inn, was demolished in 1977 in spite of local opposition. What a wasted opportunity! Ilfracombe could have been restored as a Victorian Resort, complete with a music hall and horse-drawn carriages. Instead, though the harbour remains one of the prettiest in Europe, the place looks tarnished and forlorn, a resort which has known jollier times.

Further down the North Devon coast is the most eccentric resort of all – Westward Ho!, named after a book and surely the only town in the world that boasts an exclamation mark. It, too, has had to fight for survival.

Charles Kingsley was far from honoured when they decided to exploit the title of his novel, refusing to set foot there. 'How goes the Northam Burrows Scheme for spoiling that beautiful place with hotels and villas?' he enquired of a friend in 1864. 'You will frighten away all the seapies and defile the Pebble Ridge with chicken bones and sandwich scraps.' Using 'cockney' as a term of abuse, he concluded: 'The universe is growing cockney, and men like me must look out for a new place to live in, without fear of railways and villa projection.'

The private company which raised the capital to transform seventy-five acres of farmland into a 'fashionable watering-place' included Lord Portsmouth as one of the principal investors. 'It is not too much to expect,' he announced as he laid the foundation stone, 'that a second Torquay will arise in North Devon,' and gave it the name of the 'Queen of the North Coast'.

A railway station was eventually built, and visitors were welcomed by Jolly Dutch Entertainers and Clog Dancers on the platform. A 'Royal' golf-course was built on the Burrows, where Douglas Fairbanks Senior and Mary Pickford later played. In 1899 Rudyard Kipling, who went to the United Services College on the hill, immortalised the school in *Stalky & Co*. But the College was not really top-drawer, and a feeling of coming second seems to have blighted Westward Ho! itself. According to Sir Angus Wilson, the Victorians would have thought it 'rumpty-foo'. Yet there was a glorious gallantry, even perversity, in creating an artificial resort without a natural harbour to protect it from the fury of the Atlantic Ocean, described by Kipling in his opening verse:

> Western wind and open surge
> Took us from our mothers;
> Flung us on a naked shore.
> Twelve bleak houses by the shore!
> 'Mid two hundred brothers.

This bravado was exemplified by the obligatory pier, that Victorian folly which hovered ornately, head-in-air above the sea, with glass-covered amusement domes. Was it the thrill of being over the water that made it so exciting, or the practical hope of linking rail and sea passenger services from London to Cork? In either case, it was madness. The pier was constructed in the summer, extending 600 feet into the sea, a delicate edifice on cast-iron pillars which snapped like 'tobacco pipes' when the towering lines of surf swept in with the first October storm. Against all odds the pier was finally opened two years later, together with the Nassau Bath. Aquatic entertainments were provided by the Beckwith family. The pier sported a Monster Picnic, with 1,000 seats; a rocket display; a ship in distress; and a quadrille band on the pier head in the evening.

Five years later, the Atlantic grew tired of such impertinence and smashed it to pieces in another winter storm. A scattering of iron stems can still be seen at low tide. Whenever I pass them on the coastal path to Peppercombe, I stop to admire these symbols for they reflect that yearning for new horizons and defiance of our weather, as musicians play on the beach in coats, and old ladies sport tiny 'Kiss Me Quick' hats.

British gallantry at the seaside: the local band serenades the surfers
on Woolacombe Sands in North Devon on a chilly summer's day.

I love the ugly town, especially on a shuttered winter's day when the sun spotlights the white façades with the promise of fun in the summer. Westward Ho! has one of the finest beaches in Britain and when the sun does come out the sands are crowded with laughing children, barking dogs, and young men in brand new swimming trunks gingerly testing the waves with surf-boards. Westward Ho! regains her raffish jauntiness.

Tiger Bay

Before the Race Relations Act made race relations worse, communities existed in Britain which proved that people of different colours and creeds could live together harmoniously. Tiger Bay in the Cardiff dockside was especially heartening.

When I went there towards the end of the 1950s, the district had an exotic beauty with peeling façades and a sense of former splendour. The streets were named after women: Sophia Street; Maria Street; and Alice Street, and the boats that lay on the cracked mud of low tide with the Bristol Channel beyond proved to be derelict and filled with weeds. Tiger Bay's fighting days were over.

Instead, the streets were alive with smiling people, a final glow before the place was diminished by new planning. This was the most integrated place I had been to in Britain, with Muslims, West Indians, Somalis and Arabs, even a Spanish population in a section known as 'Little Madrid'. The people looked relaxed, sitting in doorways, talking the time away or playing dice on the pavement. Coloured men improvised to guitars and a double-bass in a pub, and half-naked boys sucked ice-lollies in the sun. Best of all was the sight of children running about the streets in Muslim costume during the lengthy celebrations at the end of Ramadan, when they were given special leave of absence from school.

This was the antidote to the tension in Smethwick, Wolverhampton and Notting Hill, places which were becoming scenes of racial conflict. There was no self-consciousness because there was no awareness of being 'different'. Children of different religions played together; young men and women of different colours got married. This was the only place where I heard people refer to themselves as 'half-caste' as a matter of fact:

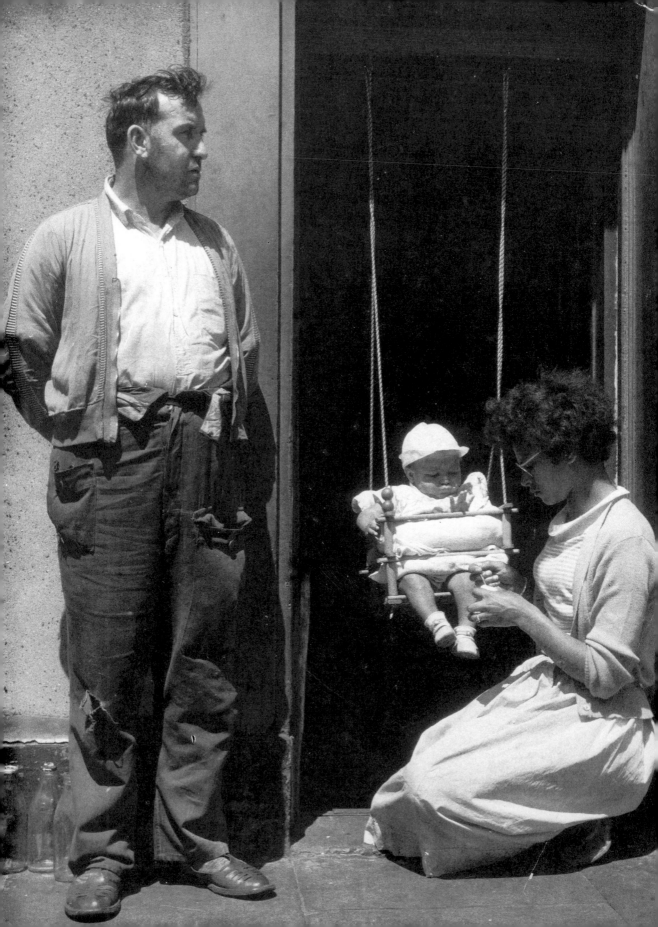

'When we leave Cardiff and someone calls us black, it's colour prejudice. If someone calls us a black bastard here, it's a straightforward insult.'

I asked an Arab if he considered himself Arab or Welsh, and he told me: 'Neither. I consider myself cosmopolitan.'

And when I asked a boy what nationalities they had at school, he listed them punctiliously in a lilting Welsh accent: 'Egyptian, African, Norwegian . . . and *Welsh!*'

This was the nature of Tiger Bay before it was tamed.

Forgotten People

Thirty years ago there were 30,000 gypsies in England, the strangers among us whom nobody cared for, preferring the name of 'travellers', for this is what we compelled them to be. Reflecting a general prejudice, a woman agreed that they did no harm, adding, 'Only it's not very nice that we are living near them.'

'Why not?'

''Cos they're dirty.'

I met a gypsy boy who was beaten up every morning on the way to his new school if he failed to give his attackers money, yet his father had fought for England: 'They treated me decent when I was in the Army,' the man told me, 'but since then I have been treated like a dog, worse than a dog because a dog has one place to stay and I can't stay nowhere. Only an hour ago the police came again and wanted me to move again. It goes on from day to day and it will be the same until I die and then maybe they will leave me in peace . . . No, sir, they don't treat us fairly. Look what this country does for those abroad, but it does nothing for us. We are the forgotten people.'

The Blaskets: The Happiest People in the World?

A small fishing trawler took us to the Blasket Islands, the last point in Europe before America. In the quiet of that evening on the journey back to Dingle, each returned with a different impression of these lonely islands.

One man found them depressing: 'I hope I never see them again.' Another thought they were haunted by ghosts; while, to another, the ruins were as impersonal as those of Pompeii – 'If only there had been some sign that human beings had lived there, a scrap of faded wallpaper or a photograph, then I might have felt something.' I agreed with Sean O'Briain, whose grandmother had taught on the Great Blasket. He was rapturous: 'If heaven is anything like this, I'll be happy to settle there.'

For me this was a journey fulfilled. One hot evening the previous year, I had seen those silhouettes from the mainland, basking on a silver sea, and I was entranced. All the more so when my companion told me of the unusual people who lived there until the last islander was forced to leave in 1954. He urged me to read *Twenty Years A'Growing*, Maurice O'Sullivan's account of his boyhood on the Great Blasket, and I became convinced that my father must have known this book, might even have travelled to the islands himself, for the simple life of the islanders epitomised everything that he admired.

I thought I knew all of my father's books in the Grey House in North Devon, which I had inherited, but my search was rewarded when I found it at last on a dark top shelf under the stairs, dusty and undisturbed, a splendid first edition translated from the Gaelic. What a rare, victorious treat it is when an author takes you into another world and shuts out the present, and O'Sullivan did this for me. His book is a surge of innocence before he grew up and his own life became muddy. This is the only book by which he is remembered, and probably the only one he wrote, for after he left the Blaskets he joined the Irish police force and died mysteriously by drowning.

In his introduction, E. M. Forster wrote of O'Sullivan's classic with surprising emotion for such an austere man, comparing it to the freshness of the egg of a seabird: 'lovely, perfect and laid this very morning'.

My instinct that my father had possessed the book had been confirmed; now I was doubly convinced that my father had travelled to the Blaskets himself, though he had never mentioned them to me. I searched for proof in his albums of old press-cuttings, finding it at last in the yellowing newsprint of the *Chicago Daily News* for 1928. O'Sullivan had left the islands a year before, leaving his dog behind him: 'Out on the bank howling as she saw me departing from her. I crushed down the distress that was putting a cloud on my heart.'

My father sailed to the Great Blasket in order to meet the king, only to discover that he had left for the mainland to collect the post. The king was also the postmaster. So my father waited for the king's return:

> Then I saw some black canoes putting out ...
>
> An hour passed and they were under our cliffs, and then a man came up the path. He was dressed in a 'swally-tail' blue coat and wore a flat black felt hat.
>
> 'The King,' said someone.
>
> He was a fine king! He had a grand face, broad and big, pale with red freckles and bright blue eyes. Or were they grey? Because it was his smile that held you most. He had lived on this tiny island all his life and so had his father before him; and yet, when he laughed, it was the laugh of a man who knew the world. He told me that when Lindbergh crossed Ireland he passed overhead. He saw him! I wonder if Lindbergh knew that the first king he saw was Patrick Kane?

I was determined to follow in my father's footsteps – as so often before – and had the luck to go there in 1970.

The fishing boat sauntered out of Dingle in the morning, a bustling village with a long quayside of coloured houses and shops with bars inside, built in a long line. The journey takes one and a half hours, past Ventry Bay, Dunquin and Eagle Mountain, pure elation unless obscured by the white, wet mist which clings interminably. On the rare hot day, the cascade of mountains runs like waves from Mount Brandon to the north, with hills that might be alpine except for that vivid Irish green and the wild red banks of fuchsia. It is a surprising landscape, for the Macgillicuddy Reeks, on the southern side of the peninsula are a smouldering blue like a distant, barren outline, and everywhere you look there is the sea, at times as blue and breathless as the Aegean.

There are six islands in the Blaskets, with the Great Blasket as the most important. Depending on the angle you see it from, the island reclines on the water like a floating man. The Great Blasket is unique, for three good reasons: this pin-point of a place produced three remarkable writers – O'Sullivan; Tomas Ò Crohan who wrote *The Islandman* 'to set down the character of the people about me so that some record of us might live after us, for the like of us will never be again'; and Peig Sayers, one of the famous Gaelic story-tellers who was born in Dunquin on the mainland in 1873 but married an islander and stayed on the Great Blasket for the rest of her life: 'I never met my husband till the day I married him, but it was a love-match till the day he died. And why shouldn't it, for he was a fine big man.'

It was grey and overcast that morning, but Sean O'Briain, who was born on the mainland, pointed out the few discernible landmarks with infectious pride. Manager of a mundane clothing store in O'Connell Street in Dublin, he returned here whenever possible; a teetotaller, he was intoxicated by this part of Ireland.

These waters have some of the best fishing in Europe but they are dangerous; a sudden swell can lift a boat up and suck it down swiftly on to a rock concealed the moment before. Sean pointed to a solitary rock where the *Santa Maria,* separated from the Armada, was dashed to pieces and sank to the bottom. It is known respectfully as the 'auld one', and fishermen threw plugs of tobacco into the sea as they sailed past in order to placate 'him'.

Because it was so abundant, it took years before the islanders realised the value of the seafood around them, but when they saw the fishermen from the mainland making big money they joined in the game. So did the French, sending their boats to buy the lobsters at ten shillings a dozen, paying a pound for a hundred of the much-despised mackerel.

High-necked cormorants surveyed the scene, apparently unconcerned by the prize of five shillings for every bird shot. 'Doesn't seem right,' said the trawlerman. 'A rod, yes, but not a gun in the boat. And they're only after the fish like we are. What have we got that's so great that they haven't?'

Around Slea Head to Dunquin and then the three-and-a-half miles to the Great Blasket. There is no landing stage, so the trawler anchored outside. It was sufficiently calm to let the rowboat glide between two fingers of rock so that we could jump on to the roughly hewn quay, but the swell can be so dangerous that two or three weeks go by before a landing is possible. All the time, as we rowed in, my eyes were held by the ruined shells of the dwellings above. Can ruins convey a former happiness? Because of O'Sullivan, they did for me, for he had described one of the finest, self-contained communities in the world.

People say that the Great Blasket is the top of a mountain sticking out of the sea, but it did not seem like that at all. The scene was slightly unreal, almost pastoral, though austere. Grey ruins against green slopes, and fields of moss and wild flowers so soft that I walked across them barefoot. There are no rats nor snakes but sheep stared at me perplexed. Looking around, I saw there were rabbits everywhere, poised in surprise, their ears twitching, so unafraid that you could catch them with your bare hands, if you were quick.

Below these fields, on the way to Blind Cove Spit and Yellow Island, lies the White Strand – a strip of sandy beach. I watched the passage of a seal across the bay and climbed down to share the pale, cool water, unaware that a shark's fin had been noticed cutting through the surface a few minutes earlier. The Strand is quiet now except for the rhythmic collapse of the surf on the sand. Once it rang with action. Sheep were driven here for shearing and islanders collected the black seaweed for manure. Every tide brought an offering. Tomas Ò Crohan remembered the day when a school of porpoises was driven on to the shore and 'everybody you saw was crimson with blood instead of being pale or swarthy. The islanders had no lack of pork for a year and a day after that.'

Above all, the Strand attracted wreckage. When I looked at the map it was easy to understand how ships were blown in by the storms and broke apart on the rocks to spill their contents on the sand. It may have meant death to the foreign sailors but gave new life to the island. When Crohan was a boy he was told of the great 'wheatship', no vestige of canvas left except for a rag on the foremast, which was blown ashore. People claimed they had never seen a wilder day and all the crew were lost, but the sacks of wheat saved the islanders in the worst year of the famine – 'If it hadn't been for her, not a soul would have survived.' The wheat that had spilled from the sacks was washed in spring water to get rid of the salt and dried in the sun. The islanders boiled it into a thick mash: 'I used to hear the old hag saying to my mother, again and again, that she never lived better in her life than the time it lasted. It was said she chewed the cud like a cow.'

Wrecks were so numerous in the First World War that some of the islanders grew rich, making hundreds of pounds by selling the goods they salvaged from ships like *The Quebra*. 'The sea filled up with everything eye had ever seen and that we had never seen in this place,' Crohan recalled, such as brass bolts and lumps of palm-oil. 'I often heard with my own ears the old hag over the way saying that God himself sent that ship amongst the poor. They lived well enough for a year or two because of her when the whole countryside on the mainland was famishing in extremity.' In their ignorance, one substance washed ashore was used as dye – their first experience of tea.

Because they were so isolated, their lives were rich in all the basic emotions – love, fear, humour, happiness and grief. Ò Crohan's first son was killed at the age of eight when he fell over the cliff, and Peig Sayer's son Tom also fell on to the rocks below; he was so battered that when he was brought home his body could not be shown publicly. Remembering how she had shaped the head back to the semblance of a skull, she made the simple comment: 'It was difficult. Let everyone carry his cross.'

Yet there were days of pure elation too, when the islanders knew a contentment denied to those in towns. Ò Crohan remembered the calm: 'You would be sitting here on a day of sun, and the water moving on the rocks and the trawlers from Dingle sailing the bay, and you would say to yourself that there was no place more beautiful in the world, east and west.' After a hard winter when they were 'hemmed in like a flock of sheep in a pen, buffeted by storm and gale, without shade or shelter', Peig Sayers welcomed the first warm weather: 'The sea is polished, and the boys are swimming down at the shore. The little fishes themselves are splashing on top of the water and even the old people are sitting out here and there sunning themselves.' Peig was canny enough to know that she was lucky: 'Many an old woman in Ireland had a nicer place and more pleasant to study than this, but I prefer this lonely place to any other in Ireland. The golden mountains of Ireland are without mist before me. The sea is pouring itself against the rocks and running in dark ravines and caves where the seal lives. We are not disturbed by the uproar and noise of the city.'

Differences would be forgotten in the midst of a sudden adventure, like the summer evening when a great shoal of mackerel swam towards them. O'Sullivan describes how the men rowed swiftly out with their nets, while the women hurried to the top of the cliffs where they screamed directions at their husbands below:

> There was not an old woman in the village but was already there, sitting on her haunches looking out at the curraghs.
>
> The evening was very still. It was a fine sight to look towards the shore of Yellow Island at the shoals of mackerel and the curraghs running round on them like big black flies.
>
> There was no misunderstanding the old women, who were foaming at the mouth with their roaring.
>
> 'Your soul to the defil,' cried one to her husband, 'throw the head of your net behind them!'
>
> 'Musha, you're my love for ever, Dermod!' cried another when she saw her husband making a fine haul of fish. One woman, Kate O'Shea, her hair streaming in the wind like a mad woman's, was screaming: 'The devil take you, Tigue, draw in your nets and go west to the south of the Sound where you will get fish for the souls of the dead. Och, my pity to be married to you . . .'

Many thousands of mackerel were caught that night. But when O'Sullivan was old enough to join the fishermen, he confided to his grandfather after his first day: 'I think, Daddo, there is nothing so bad as fishing.'

'You may be sure of it, my bright love.'

O'Sullivan was making fun of his dissatisfaction, yet he was one of many islanders who were losing their enchantment with this simple way of life. One day he told his father that he was leaving:

> He looked into the fire, thinking. At last he looked up: 'Are you in earnest?'
>
> 'I am indeed.'
>
> 'When will you be going?' said he with a sigh.
>
> 'Tomorrow.'
>
> 'Well, I give you my blessing, for so far as this place is concerned there is no doubt but it has gone to ruin.'

Island life had become too hard, too narrow for the young people, who hankered after shops and amusements. Undeniably, the life was poor. The houses were only ten to twenty feet long and, in Ò Crohan's case, so close together that if 'the old hag' had wanted to, 'she could have scalded my mother from her own doorway with boiling water'. Apart from a spinning-wheel, the only decorations were holy pictures and portraits of national heroes, or washed-up light-bulbs used as ornaments. Much of the furniture was made from wrecks. A partition divided the houses in two – on one side were the beds, with sacks of potatoes stored underneath and barrels of salt fish in the corner; on the other side was the kitchen, where the family passed the time. At night they must have gasped for space and air, especially in the winter when they shared it with a cow and a calf, an ass, two or three dogs and a pet lamb. If the grandparents were alive, they slept on the floor near the warmth of the turf fire, puffing away at their clay pipes. In the niche beside the chimney there might have been a cat, and kittens. A pot hung above the hearth. The roofs were made of thatch and children scrambled on top to collect the eggs that the hens laid in the rush. Later the roofs were made of tarred felt, and the animals kept outside in a separate shed. No wonder that all the family, especially the children, welcomed the coming of spring and football in the fields. Life depended on the seasons.

But though their winter existence sounds stifling to us today, they had the distraction of story-tellers like Peig Sayers, with nightly dancing in the larger houses. There was even a special house where boys and girls could stay until midnight, and Ò Crohan recorded with satisfaction that 'Nothing wrong ever happened among them for the sixty-seven years that I've known it.' Without such discipline, life would have unravelled.

There are signs that people lived on the Blaskets a thousand years ago. Some ancient race built a fort on the summit, then the Danes invaded, and a tower dating from the French wars stood intact until it was shattered by a thunderbolt.

After the First World War 250 people were left on the island, 1,000 sheep, thirty cows and twenty-nine horses, whose foals were swum across the bay when the weather was calm to be sold on the mainland. Eighty children went to school and they learnt enough to leave for America, sending back the money for the fares of their younger brothers and sisters. After the Second World War the decline was swift and the last islander, as I have said, was obliged to leave in 1954.

On my visit sixteen years later the island was inhabited again, by two men who were passing the summer in one of the shell-like houses – a teacher from Dublin, who was born on the Great Blasket, and his uncle who was eighty-seven. There was a splendid sympathy between them. The old man had been born on the island, too, and though he spent many of his years in America, he had reverted to his Gaelic tongue and his nephew acted as interpreter. This annual return to his birthplace was the incentive that kept him alive.

At first the old man was too shy to meet me, due to an ugly ear-infection, but then he relaxed and invited me into the bare stone house with whitewashed walls. There he told me about the king, and his role as spokesman of the island, and the sheep and even cattle brought from the mainland in their slender curraghs. The concept of a cow in such a deli-

cate craft seemed incredible, for one kick would have shattered the fabric of wooden slats and tarred canvas, but the animal lay on its back, its feet bound, on a bed of bracken, too terrified to move. Even so . . .

One point still puzzles me: why were the cows taken to the mainland for mating? Surely a bullock was sometimes born after their return? The old man doubted if there ever was a bull, perhaps too violent a beast for such a small community.

The absence of a church was harder to explain. Apparently there was a small grave-yard, submerged by now, for stillborn children and the decomposed bodies of sailors washed ashore. Twice a year the priest would come over to say Mass in the school-house, but when an islander died his body was taken to the mainland in a funeral cortège, as many as eighteen curraghs drifting across the bay beside it. Burials and marriages were performed in the old church at Ballyferriter, and Ò Crohan writes about the cele-brations in the pub after either event:

> There was no silent drinking then. There would be as many as twenty men in
> the room drinking, and every man that came in he would not go out without
> singing a song or telling a tale. And you would go down into the street, there
> would be noise coming out of another tavern and it would be the same there,

tales-a-telling and songs-a-singing and no man quiet. There were four pubs in Ballyferriter, each with a fiddler of its own, and many of the guests ended the wedding night in hospital.

Ò Crohan added the crucial comment: 'You would hear no word of English.'

In the times of the troubles, the Great Blasket was a place of refuge for the Gaelic tradition. The island fulfilled a spiritual purpose. Were the islanders nobler because of this? Had they really been an exceptional race or had I romanticised them? Were they, in fact, much the same as the people in any small village on the mainland at the time?

I asked these questions at Tom Long's pub back in Dingle that night, and he took me to see one of the surviving islanders who lived nearby. Sean Kearney had a brick-red complexion and laughed hugely at the end of every sentence, possibly because our talk was so bizarre: we spoke in English but our accents were so foreign to each other that Long's ten-year-old-son had to act as interpreter.

Three Kearney brothers had sailed from Ventry and settled on the Blaskets four hundred years ago. The islanders were as happy as anyone in the world, he told me, just as the rabbits are today. 'Any place where you are born is all right, but we had dancing *every* night and playing cards, and visitors in the summer, English, German, Irish, all come to speak Gaelic . . . It was fishing and work all day and happy in the night. Everyone was busy keeping everyone else.'

'Why?' I asked deceptively.

'We *had* to!' and he gave a thunderous laugh. 'We want you tomorrow but you may want me the day after.'

His father had been the postman, although never the king, going to the mainland three times a week for a salary of a pound. Sean himself was the last postmaster in 1940, when there was a radio link with the mainland.

I was curious about what they ate on the island.

'Potatoes, three times a day. Soup off the rabbits. No flour, no sugar, no tea. In old days we'd make our own butter and put it into a bog and keep it for ever. My grandfather was ninety-nine years old; if you gave him a sweet cake he'd throw it between your two eyes.'

After potatoes, fish was the staple diet, especially boiled mackerel, salted down for the winter. The chickens who nested in the roofs were no good, Sean declared. 'I'd rather a sea-bird, rather a puffin or a seagull if they're young. Boy, they're good! Rather a puffin than any steak.'

He told me he believed in fairies, unless he was telling me what I wished to hear, the bedevilling courtesy of the Irish. 'The old people heard them every night, singing and crying . . .

'They're not there now, there's too much traffic in the world.' He gave another hoot of laughter. 'When I was seventeen, I came back from fishing and saw a lady standing near the house and she was as white as snow, and out of her mouth a flame. "What's wrong with you?" asked my father. "Look," I said, "look, see that." Boy, he crossed himself, he always carried holy water and sprinkled it just in case. She disappeared and we went home and we were sweating. Sweating in bed I was, and we'd had no porter that day!'

I asked the question which worried me: 'What was the difference between the islanders and those on the mainland?'

He gave a delightful grin: 'We were like fish out there, oh so lively! On the mainland they were snails.'

The next morning, as bright as any day in *Twenty Years A'Growing*, I drove to Bally-ferriter in search of another islander, Tom Daly, and found him with his brother and two affectionate sheepdogs in their garden, with a tremendous sweep of fields behind them and the Blaskets in the distance. Daly was the last craftsman to make the black curraghs, which he called *naovogs*. Once they were built to hold a crew of eight, then four became common, now Daly's boats seated three. Seeing them close to, it seemed impossible that such a delicate framework could support anything at all, especially in winter storms, yet they had proved the strongest craft of all and Daly, who was born on the Great Blasket in 1900, could not remember a single death by drowning. Like the canoes they resembled, their lightness made them easy to manoeuvre between the rocks, though the islanders tied a bottle of holy water and a medal on the prow for good measure. I was surprised to find his workshop bare except for a few basic tools – a grindstone, axe and plane. His eye, his touch, his natural skill provided the rest.

Back in Tom Long's pub that night, Mrs Long told me that Tom Daly's father had been famous for the fine violins he made: 'He was a lovely old man. He had a culture and a kindness, something you don't find every day. And he was popular.' She was a teacher, helping out in her husband's pub during the holidays, and she gave me the name of the last teacher on the Great Blasket – Mary Fitzgerald, now Mrs O'Brian. I traced her the next evening in a small fishing village near Kenmare. She welcomed me with surprise: 'You're the first man who has spoken to me of the Blaskets since I left.'

There were thirty-three pupils when she arrived in 1934 and only nine when she left in 1940. They were more sophisticated than the children in Ò Crohan's time, who had screeched and roared with laughter when the School Inspector came from the mainland – he was the first man they had seen wearing spectacles.

Gaelic was forbidden on the Irish mainland by order of the British, and a child could be punished if caught reading a Gaelic book. But the Blaskets lived by their own laws, and English was the difficult subject to teach.

She also remembered Tom Daly's father's musical genius: 'Once he visited Innish Tooshkert, one of the other Blasket Islands, and thought he heard the fairies playing a tune which he memorised and played to the islanders afterwards. They called it The Fairy Tune. It was very sorrowful.'

'Did any of the islanders want to leave in 1954?'

'Oh, they did! You see it was the old story of the young people wanting to improve themselves. They were more aware of the dangers of life than the older generation of fishermen, and they did not seem so skilled any more.'

This is the pattern of the Blasket Islands, a loss of the old skills, rejection of the

simpler way of life in the name of progress, the father stronger than the son. Before I left, I visited Ò Crohan's grave near Dunquin, dark and overgrown, with the Blaskets dominating the horizon, as they always seem to do from the mainland. The Gaelic inscription quotes his prophesy - 'The like of us will never be again' – and that is the way it should be. The island itself could be 'improved' but the people can never be replaced. 'They were the happiest in the world,' Mrs Long told me, and their happiness came from inside themselves. Brendan Behan never landed there, but he watched them from Dunquin and their loneliness inspired his poem *The Jackeen's Lament for the Blaskets*. It is written in Gaelic and dedicated to Sean O'Briain, my companion when we sailed from Dingle, with whom he shared a cell in Mountjoy Prison. This is the first verse of Brendan's poem, translated by the late Donagh MacDonagh:

> The sea will be under the sun like an empty mirror,
> No boat under sail, no sign of a living sinner
> And nothing reflected but one golden eagle, the last
> On the edge of the world beyond the lonely Blaskets.

The New Australians

When I returned to Australia in 1961, the contrast with my arrival on the *Orcades* a few years earlier was striking. This time I was a 'star'. A spurious sort of star, admittedly, a so-called TV personality. The likes of Alan Whicker and Cliff Michelmore had not been seen on Australian television, and even Richard Dimbleby was barely familiar, but my programmes had been shown regularly on ABC. With the hope of further exchange, Associated-Rediffusion sent me out to film a series of thirteen stories in the six Australian states, eventually transmitted as *Farson in Australia*. We had a local camera crew, even an accountant with the delightful if misleading name of Bob Wealthy. I flew out with a script-writer, and the director with whom I worked most closely, a wonderful, gifted, humorous man – the late Rollo Gamble.

Grounded at Rome, we missed our connection for Perth in Singapore and were re-routed via Sydney, a mere 5,000 miles of extra flying time.

Until then the flight had been exhausting – an endless cocktail party without friends – but as we flew south from Darwin I became awestruck, almost subdued by the limitless space, mile after empty mile, hour after hour, without any sign of man, or of a road across the dry, veined landscape, broken only where water flowed a million years ago. Rollo described our arrival in his report to the company.

> It was frightfully hot, we were sweating copiously . . . I remember David's shirt, a sort of poison-bottle green with great black patches of his sweat. My own state was hardly more attractive and Dan, I think, had gone into some sort of mystic trance induced by heat and boredom. We longed for a taste of

the famed Australian beer at Sydney airport, with a shower and a shave to freshen us for the 2,500 miles to Perth, but this was not to be. Three dishevelled 200 pounders were seized by a pack of journalists, their bags thrown at the customs man, who was hardly given time to make his chalk mark, and ushered upstairs to a private room with a trestle table loaded with drink. Thank God, in a way – but no wash and shave. Thank God, they were only interested in Dan who, already at the point of exhaustion, was interviewed, photographed, and filmed until he was almost fit for the undertaker.

The barrage of questions from the rows of smart, tough journalists included 'Are you here to shock us?'

'No, we simply wish to record some impressions,' I replied, adding, with a feeble smile, that we might produce 'one or two tiny shocks in the process'.

The headline the next morning was *Farson Here To Shock Us* which was what they wished to hear.

The most frequent question I was asked over the next few months was 'How do you like Australia?' I remembered the Australians' constant need for reassurance – they are hard yet genteel, with a streak of puritanism lurking below the brashness – so I refrained from saying I found it an open-hearted nation with a chip on its shoulder, a healthy dislike

for authority and work, and an admiration for the man 'who gets away with it'. I settled for unqualified approval, because I did not want to sit in judgement, like the type of reporter so detested by my father, who travelled through Russia in a train 'with the blinds pulled down' and then published a book entitled *My Life with the Soviets*. Only at the end of my journey did I dare venture: 'There's not enough *wrong* with you.' And the Australians did not know what to make of that.

Our brief was not to concentrate on the outback, which was too obvious, but to reveal any sophistication we could find in the cities to appease the Australian neurosis of being thought uncultured. Yet it was the sophistication of the outback and remoter regions, the directness of people there who cannot be bothered to pretend, be they the no-hopers or prospectors for gold, that I was to find exhilarating. In spite of the flight from Darwin, which looked as if I had come to the end of the earth rather than the beginning, thirty years ago Australia had the vigour of youth. The photographs I took in 1961 are now in the State Library of New South Wales, acquired as a record of the period because the changes have taken place so rapidly.

Rich Dirt and Ghost Towns

The approach to Kalgoorlie could not be described as pretty, through identical miles of disheartening scrub known aptly as mongrel-mulga, yet the land had a certain grandeur. The town was scarred by the Golden Mile and dominated by a slag-heap like a miniature but unmysterious Ayers Rock. I referred to it as 'one of the most godforsaken spots on earth', which earned me a rebuke in the local *Commerce, Industrial and Mining Review*, yet the area symbolised romance at the turn of the century. Though it was parched and pitted now, with deep cracks like running sores, and defeated thistles the only vegetation, the residents spoke of it proudly as 'the richest square mile on earth'.

The 'gold-rush' began when an Irishman called Patrick Hannan rode out from Coolgardie with his two partners, Flanagan and Shea. Searching for their pack-horse, which wandered away, and fresh water, Hannan made his find on 15 June 1893. In the next few days they discovered 100 ounces of gold. As there were rival prospectors in the area, they agreed to send Hannan back to Coolgardie twenty miles away to file his reward claim with the warden. The great gold-rush was on.

In a few years the population of Western Australia had doubled and by 1901 the Golden Mile had yielded more than 70 million tons of ore and 32 million ounces of gold.

Camp followers and Afghan traders who rode camels joined the hundreds of men who swarmed to 'the new place'. A new arrival from South Australia described the activity in Coolgardie: 'So much bustle and hurry; so many men in a hurry! The wide street crowded with riding horses, horses harnessed in drays and buggies, camels in buckyards: men on foot and even men with wheelbarrows: all going for their lives . . . !' Entertainers stood on tables and sang to the miners in the saloons, and the atmosphere was that in the Klondike – of hope, extravagance, greed and bitter disappointment.

At first 'the new place' was known as Hannan's until it was changed by poll in 1895 to Kalgoorlie, derived from the aboriginal Kalgurli. When I arrived in 1961 Paddy Hannan's statue, complete with his precious water-bottle, still dominated the main street. Hannan's Modern Lounge nearby boasted the slogan 'Say Hannan's. Like Gold, Sets the Standard', which was echoed in smaller letters on the Oriental Hotel. I relished these hotels with their covered arcades at street level to shut out the sun, elaborate, cast-iron balustrades above, and high, broad windows to encourage every breath of air.

Prostitutes had moved into Hay Street during the gold rush. Incredibly, they were still there, and judging by the glimpses I caught through the wooden bars they might be aged remnants of that first, rich flush. I assumed they were kept behind bars by law, but an old-timer, a spry, sardonic old man with a head as bald and oval as an egg, assured me that it was to protect them from trouble-makers. They did not require a licence and the police left them alone. Even so, it seemed strange to see a row of brothels in such ghostly circumstances.

During the *Poseidon* bonanza a few years later, when they found nickel forty miles away, the ladies of Hay Street enjoyed a popularity which they never dreamt would come their way again. For a short time they were back in business, and some were able to retire, at last, to a genteel suburb in the south.

In 1903 the formidable gold-fields water scheme piped water all the way from Perth. Until then water was so scarce it cost as much as beer, two shillings for a gallon of brackish liquid taken from the ground, steamed and condensed. This was why, they say, the flashy landlord of the United Service Hotel in Coolgardie used to bathe in champagne. Mrs McCall, an old lady in her nineties, remembered scrubbing Paddy Hannan's back in her grandmother's lodging house in Perth when he came back from the gold-fields: 'He hadn't had a bath for months and he stank.'

The old-timer saw the water turned on in Kalgoorlie: 'Why, I reckon that was the best day we've ever seen. Everybody went to the bars and got drunk. They also got shot.' The old man chuckled.

It is easy to understand the excitement – the temperature was 103 on the day the scheme opened, and rose to 114 degrees over the next few days. By 1961 Kalgoorlie boasted an Olympic swimming pool holding half a million gallons of water. It cost three million pounds to build, a staggering sum at the time, until you realise that the gold strike yielded five hundred million. In spite of this, Hannan ended up as a poor man, existing on £150 a year donated by the state. Another man, Oliver Page, found two mines and ran through two fortunes.

'Drink and dice and two-up all the rest of it,' said the old-timer, sitting in a broken chair outside his dilapidated wooden shack. 'Everybody was friendly, they wouldn't see a person hard up or wanting a feed or nothing, yet I think gold is one of the most foolish occupations in the world. Here we are digging it out of the ground and then we send it across the world to Fort Knox where it gets buried again. Yep, a sort of madness, and all that glitters 'tis not gold,' he added gravely. 'Take the Bardock murder: one man at the bot-

tom of the shaft, some fifty feet down, sent up a bucket of shiny ore. Now the fellow at the top was obsessed with the idea of making millions of pounds and thought this was gold. So what did he do? Start dropping rocks on his mate in the shaft. Thought he'd killed him, but he hadn't . . . Bardock, crushed and fly-blown, crawled to the surface and managed to accuse his murderer before he died. Anyway, it wasn't gold at all.'

Then there was the Cemetery Rush in 1897 in Kanowna, when a vein of gold was found running underneath the graveyard. At first the authorities were adamant that no prospecting could be allowed, but they had to yield to pressure and declare the ground free for pegging. At two o'clock on a scorching afternoon in December, hundreds of prospectors lined up with spades outside. When the police sergeant dropped a white handkerchief they fought their way in. It took weeks to sort out their claims among the broken tombstones, and it was then discovered that the vein had petered out.

By 1961 Kanowna was a ghost town. Sixteen hotels and two breweries had flourished in the gold rush; now there were only a few signposts marking the former streets, and a few stones overgrown by grass swept flat by the wind – the tombstones perhaps?

Coolgardie was heading the same way, with crumbling façades and a dwindling population of a few hundred compared to twenty thousand at its peak. To escape the melancholy, the blinding sun, and the persistence of an aged, ragged Aboriginal, I sought refuge in a hotel (the fancy word for a pub). There was a choice of two: the Railway (surely inappropriate) and the Denver City, which sounded equally bizarre.

In the Denver City I found the Otters seated at the bar.

The Two Otters

When I asked for a schooner of beer, my unadulterated English accent ricocheted in the cavernous silence. The older Otter beckoned me over and shook my hand, explaining that he had served in the British Navy until 1924. An Englishness lingered, though his son was typically Australian – he wore a white vest over hard brown skin and uttered such laconic remarks as 'My word!' and 'That's for sure!'

The Otters were lone prospectors and the father's motive had a beautiful logic. He was a lighthouse keeper so heartily sick of the sea that when he went on leave he tried to get as far away from it as possible. The former gold-fields provided the perfect antidote, and prospecting was their passion. Father Otter described it as 'a bit like fishing'.

We talked of England and drank, and when it was time for them to leave, they invited me to join them. I climbed into their splendid 1928 open Rugby among the picks and shovels and we set out into the bush. The Otters were working a disused mine with three shafts which they called the Three Jolly Britons. For ten shillings they had staked their claim to twelve acres and by now they were eighty feet down.

The day grew hotter. They worked with slow satisfaction, but I realised that prospecting, like fishing, demands an infinite patience. The lean and wiry son crushed the stone – 'It's a poor man who can't crush eight tons a day' – while the father washed it, peering at the pan through a magnifying glass. He showed me a few grains of glistening yellow and reckoned that by the end of their holiday they would have collected twelve ounces of gold worth more than £200: enough to cover their expenses.

The real, tantalising incentive was the hope of a strike. 'If I struck some rich dirt,' confided the son in a sudden burst of loquacity, 'we could make as much as £75,000 and then

I wouldn't be working no more and I'd take the family to see the old country, which Pa has told me of.' They admitted it was 'a mug's game', but I left two men who were blissfully content.

So, too, was Joe Orr, back at the Golden Mile. He had emigrated from Blackpool long before it sported a Golden Mile of its own. He emerged from his hole blinking like a mole and showed me the primitive hut where he lived by himself.

'I have a radio and I have a dog. I've been doing it so long it's second nature to me. As a matter of fact I couldn't put up with the hustle and bustle of a working life. I've no ambition to have a dozen things on time payment, I've no lounge suit or refrigerator but what I have is mine.' He listed his deprivations with pride.

Orr had twenty-one acres, which cost a pound a year. Like the Otters he was working an 'old show' which he was convinced held more. Already he had made enough to buy the

equipment to dig deeper and hoped to make as much as £1,500 a year. He was an optimist but had known disappointment: 'I sank a hole and couldn't get any gold. I was just about to give it away in disgust when I broke some dirt from the leader and took it over to the tub and washed it. To my astonishment I picked out six ounces of pure gold from that dish of dirt. "Well, Joe," I cried, "this is the Jackpot!" but I never got another grain of colour.'

I was beginning to understand the compulsion of gold-fever. 'It gets into your blood and you can't leave it,' he agreed, 'and you always come back. I could go to a good job tomorrow but I know I never will. I've done a lot of reading but this is better than any book. I'm always wondering what the next page is going to bring forth.'

Some people would say that Orr was mad to endure such a harsh, monotonous existence. There is an irony in the fact that he and the Otters were totally dedicated to gold, yet were the least mercenary of men.

On my last visit to Australia in October 1986 I met another man fired by mineral fever. I took a cab from Melbourne University to catch the ferry to Tasmania. As we drove off, the grizzled driver looked at me and laughed out loud. I asked what amused him so much. 'Because it's Christmas Day for me,' he cried. 'I'm chucking up this damned job at midnight and going back to the work I truly love.' He was leaving for one of the most hellish places in South Australia, the Opal mines at Andamooka, attracted by the lure of opals as the other men were by gold. The heat is so terrible above ground, rising to 140 degrees, that miners build their houses below ground, but even there the temperature is 80 degrees. They have electricity and fridges, he told me. 'A few lucky bastards have air-conditioning. We drink water all day long, and it pours off like a stream.'

The diggers work from dawn until ten o'clock, when the heat becomes unbearable and drives them underground. They re-emerge at sunset to work for another four hours. My driver was a cutter. The companies prefer the cutting to be done on the spot, for if they send a chunk of dirt away, the cutter might be tempted to keep it for himself if he finds a perfect vein inside. Yet the attraction is more than financial: 'I get my tools out and cut and polish and after a couple of hours I have a work of art. It's beautiful! You should see the changing colours.' In a smart shop in Sydney known as Opal Beauty I bought a cheap souvenir: scraps of opal in a glass phial filled up with water, and I am still entranced by the brilliance of the colours as they catch the light. You can pay up to £5,000 for a well-cut stone.

I am sure my driver was a good cutter, but he was a lousy driver. We made the ferry with a minute to spare and he refused any payment, apologising profusely for having taken the wrong turning.

'Don't worry,' I called back as I ran up the gangway with my luggage, 'remember it's Christmas Day!' He waved back joyfully, in the knowledge that he was returning to the place he loves – those diabolical opal fields where he has found romance.

Boom Town

In Kalgoorlie I looked back to the past; in Cooma I was thrust into the future. This was the heart of the hydro-electric scheme in the Snowy Mountains and Cooma was a boom town, a modern equivalent of the gold-rush towns in Western Australia. In the Snowy Mountains 20,000 men – Greeks, Poles, Yugoslavs, Czechs, Hungarians and Germans – were brought in to change the course of rivers, making them flow west instead of east in order to irrigate the land. Eight colossal dams, ten power stations, and a hundred miles of tunnel cut through the mountains, creating new lakes and drowning villages in the process. It was eerie to look down and see the steeple of a church below the water. The Snowy Mountain Scheme cost £375 million, and the men who came here hoped to make their fortunes, earning as much as £100 a day. I met one Italian who owned six trucks worth £12,000 each and claimed he made £800 a day. With little to spend their money on, they came down from their camps in the mountains to drink and gamble their wages away in the Wild-West atmosphere of Cooma, little more than a main street of banks and bars.

These were the New Australians, and I was in my element for they had stories to tell. However, there was a formidable obstacle. I needed to match them drink for drink.

I have taken part in some drinking marathons in my time, but few so tough as this. For me, one of the rewards of alcohol is the rare rapport before the euphoria and the rot. Then it is possible to achieve an intimacy with strangers which could well be denied to their families. Suspicion was overcome when they realised that I, too, was a stranger in a strange land, and once I gained their confidence I had it absolutely. I was hurled into a party which celebrated the arrival of a huge Zorba-like Greek. At first it seemed strange

to sit in a room for half-an-hour and hardly hear a word of English, but language problems were overcome by drink. Six bottles of whisky were stuck in ice-buckets and were emptied in an hour by five of us. A Spaniard passed out on the floor; Zorba danced on the table and tore off his shirt; and as we lurched past midnight I found myself in yet another bar in earnest conversation with the Australian sitting beside me. I rested my hand lightly on his knee in a spirit of comradeship as I emphasised some point. He rose with a scream of rage, prepared to hit me, but a group of Greeks bustled me out of the place like mafia-minders and back to my motel. They seemed to be telling me that the man was the assistant chief of police. He came to arrest me in the morning.

Rollo, who had taken part in the marathon drinking the night before, staggered into the dining-room for breakfast to witness an angry scene at the reception desk, where the assistant chief of police was demanding to see me. Rollo stepped in and invited the policeman to join him for coffee. When he learned I was about to be arrested, Rollo clapped his hands with pleasure. 'But that's *marvellous*!' he exclaimed. The man looked suspicious and Rollo explained: 'Frankly, and this is between us, this is just the shot in

the arm we've been needing. As you may know, Dan is a big name in England and this will cause a sensation there – and in Sydney with the ABC. Think of the wonderful publicity for Dan! And such fun when they hear of the charge.' I was told by the sound-man afterwards that Rollo's tone became grave as he continued, 'By the way, what *is* the charge? Serious, I trust?'

'Well,' the policeman mumbled, thoroughly disconcerted by now, 'he put his hand on my knee and I'm going to charge him with assault.'

As an actor *manqué* Rollo rose to the occasion. 'Your *knee?*' he exclaimed. 'This is the loveliest thing I've ever heard, we must get a photograph of the two of you together.

"My word!", as you say in Australia, I can see the headlines now. I admire your courage, sir, indeed I do.'

I gather it was a great performance. The assistant chief of police left the motel muttering dire threats should he see me again. We did meet over the next few days and he made a few half-hearted lunges, but was restrained by the Greeks and Poles who hated the man. Because of the episode we got the interviews with the migrants, who were now our friends.

Wally, the German, told me about the illegal card-games which could last for days up at Cabramurra, the highest settlement in Australia. Sometimes they used the photographs sent by would-be mail-order brides from Europe as their pack of cards. I thought the idea of proxy brides was far-fetched until I realised that the men outnumbered the women by a hundred to one, and heard that the Black Maria paid a weekly visit to the railway station to intercept the prostitutes from Sydney and send them back.

Ivan the Czech had travelled to Sydney to collect his mail-order bride, only to discover she had married a Pole on the way over. So many of the women fell in love on board ship that it was suggested that migrant ships should be restricted to one sex only. As Ivan stood disconsolately on the quayside, a woman ran up and threw her arms around him: 'Marry me, marry me, for pity's sake, marry me. I've just seen my husband and I can't stand him.' Ivan smiled nostalgically: 'We stayed together for a weekend. Not bad, but no good for wife.'

They would have liked women from their own part of the world, but in Sydney I tracked down a Bulgarian who was waiting for his Yugoslav bride, whom he had never seen. She had gone through a 'proxy' ceremony before he sent her the fare, to avoid any possible mishap on the voyage over. Milete could only just speak English but his smile was beatific in his state of anticipation.

He may not have been scared, but as we waited interminably for the Italian ship *Flamina* to dock at dawn three mornings later, I was highly nervous. Milete stood beside me in his Sunday suit, holding her photograph for identification.

The couple met at last, and embraced awkwardly. Veska Natschev turned out to be a formidable woman and my heart sank when I realised that neither spoke each other's language. She clutched a bouquet of artificial flowers, which seemed wildly inappropriate. However, in her other hand she held a bottle of Yugoslavian slivovitz, which she gave Milete on the quayside as her dowry. A good omen. I was in tears as Milete left to introduce his new wife to her new home in a new country.

Strangers in a strange land, where insurance for the Snowy Mountains Scheme allowed for the death of one man per mile in the tunnelling at Eucumbene-Tumut. I wondered romantically if their work for the future, turning dry plains into fertile land, inspired the men from different countries to work so well together. Wally the German brought me back to earth with a cynical laugh: 'You talk madness, Danny. Money is the only inspiration here.'

Even so, Rollo and I were sufficiently inspired by the project to want to make an hour-long 'special' about it. John Macmillan, the Comptroller of Programmes in London cabled this generous response: 'Your enthusiasm matched by my trust,' but Sir Eric Harrison, the Australian High Commissioner, tried to censor *Strangers in a Strange Land* before it was transmitted in England. 'I told them there was too much emphasis on sex in it,' he explained. Associated-Rediffusion agreed and it was shown 'with the worst parts taken out'.

The writer Colin MacInnes, who came from Australia, sent me a letter of support:

> It was entirely predictable that the programme's truth would be mistrusted. The sad thing is that, even by their own standards, they're *wrong*. I mean this. The revelation of today is the commonplace of tomorrow. What you have divined and revealed, they will boast about in five years' time. But today, they're scared.
>
> Your themes were: work, sex, loot, life: and what *else* can a country calling itself 'new' be, than that? But no: the idiotic H. Commissioner (good luck to him!) wants a *fragment* of that reality, wrapped up in koala bears and wattle.

Though Sir Eric condemned me for 'giving the wrong impression' of Australia, Kenneth Pearson wrote in the *Sunday Times*:

> His piece is informed with intelligence, devoid of sentimentality and delivered with the passion of a man whose interest in the subject is sincere. He is, I suspect, our alter ego; the one who does, while we sit and dream of what we'll do.
>
> *Strangers* made all TV Westerns look like so many fairy tales, when one compares their almost depersonalised heroes with these Hemingway characters who are willing to pit their own ancient culture against a raw environment in exchange for the wide open spaces and the chance to earn eighty pounds a day.

Mr Pearson understood exactly what I had been aiming for, and if it smacks of conceit to quote him, I might add that *Strangers* – along with all my films for Associated-Rediffusion – were destroyed when the company lost the franchise a few years later. His review and a few photographs help to remind me of those New Australians.

The Cattle Station

That journey around Australia was a rare reward in my television career: everything was *different*. I was astounded by the robustness of the place and the candour of the people. When I stumbled on a story about a cattle station to the north, Rollo shared my enthusiasm. After a reconnaissance trip in a tiny Cesna we returned by road from the coast of North Queensland through the rich Atherton Plateau and a countryside so stupendous that I felt elated. The immensity of the acacia trees constantly surprised me.

The journey took a mere nine hours, whereas when the first settlers came here with their cattle, it took several years. One of the earliest pioneers was a man called James Atkinson, who left the coastal town of Bowen in 1861 and settled in Wairuna. Now his descendants flourished on the homestead, 'not a big affair,' the sons had assured me – just the size of Denmark. In 1961 the nearest shop was seventy-six miles away.

For me, this was the essence of all that was good in Australia – space, simplicity, a love of nature and a zest for life.

Rollo was radiant, totally in his element, and the Australian camera crew worked from seven in the morning until midnight without complaint. This was a welcome contrast to the infuriating restrictions imposed by the unions back home. Rollo and I strove for a form of television *verité*, without the pretension this word implies, and relished our new freedom.

The patriarch of the Atkinson clan was Ken Atkinson, grandson of James, a fine, tough man. His uncle was the first white child born north of Bowen: 'He was born in the bush, and then they went on. They eventually settled on Mount Surprise. I often wondered why these old people went so far, because there must have been miles and miles of open

With Ken Atkinson and the Aboriginal Peter Wairuna at the cattle station of Wairuna in Northern Queensland.

country close to Bowen, but they seemed to want to get three, four, five hundred miles before they'd settle down. The Jardines carried on to the Cape York peninsula and if they'd gone any further they'd have ended in the sea!'

James Atkinson travelled with everything he had and about 500 cattle, and sheep. In 1881 they took up Wairuna. 'It's good cattle country, well-watered,' Ken Atkinson said. 'In those days they just turned the cattle into the bush, they didn't wander far. The saying goes that if your cattle stray, you've got to go to your neighbour's property to eat your own meat.'

When they turned them loose in this curiously haphazard way, they allowed 10 per cent natural deaths, and more were speared by the Aborigines. His grandfather had fought off several attacks.

'I think they all had to be tough to survive in those days,' he said of his grandfather. 'That's what made him come to Australia in the first place. He came from Ireland and grandmother came from Scotland, though they met and married in Victoria. I suppose he was looking for bigger opportunities and Australia certainly presented them. It used to take them six months to go back to Bowen by bullock wagon and three months to come back with food. They'd take their wool down, and sheep also. If they were attacked, he was quicker on the draw than the blacks.'

Rich cattle-owners by now, with about 8,000 head of cattle, life at Wairuna remained tough. Cattle was their passion and at night the Atkinsons talked of little else: 'It's the best time for selling we've ever known, we're on top of the boom.'

Every six weeks, 700 bullocks were rounded up and dipped. I watched them being gelded with red hot tongs, a traumatic spectacle, though the animals did not appear to suffer as much as I expected. Castrated at fourteen months, the stags – as the young

bulls now became – lost interest and kept clear of the other bulls.

Every fortnight the two Atkinson sons, Bob and John, rode round their territory to check that the fences were in order. The danger came when they had to separate the animals for the journey south to market: 'It can be frightening – 500 cattle all going one way, rushing towards you. If they hit a fence, possibly the first fifteen are crushed to death before the fence is pushed down and the rest are away. When they're unruly, we use dart tranquillisers. It's like the animal's dead for four or five minutes – a total paralysis.

'Wild horses, they're a menace and we shoot 'em,' Bob continued. 'They're fantastic fighters, once they bite they never let go and they get so darned clever they go for the knee. When the young colts grow up and start taking an interest in the mares, the stallions hunt 'em out or kill 'em, though they leave the fillies alone.'

The last of the wild Aborigines worked here. 'He was a different tribe from the ones that were here,' Ken told me. 'I had to go away for a few days and I left him with another boy who was also from a different tribe. I was careful to send the other boys in another direction. But while I was away they came in and knocked this fellow on the head and ate him . . . ate part of him anyway . . .'

'Ate him!' I echoed, incredulously. 'Did he die?'

'Oh yes, he died! He didn't die immediately but he had a great chunk of beef taken out of his back. It was a tribal thing, they thought it would make them strong, brave and good. To my knowledge, that was the last case of cannibalism in Queensland.'

Now the Aborigines lived in harmony, if not equality. Peter Wairuna had been found abandoned in the bush. The boy was named after the homestead because he had forgotten his real name. The first time he saw the sea he assumed it was fresh water and drank it 'until I couldn't take any more'. He had yet to go swimming. Neither Peter nor any of the black employees were allowed to drink the 'hard-stuff' when they were working, so they would ride into town; although the publicans were not allowed to sell liquor to an Aboriginal in Queensland, they did so under the counter.

'This is his home,' said Ken Atkinson, 'he doesn't like the noisy streets or crowds.' Peter earned approximately six pounds a week, two thirds of which went into his personal account at the Native Affairs Department. The Atkinsons regarded him with

the affection accorded to a child. They were bound together by the land. Ken's wife told me that 'an old gin', an Aboriginal woman who had been her husband's nurse when he was little, had looked after her in the early days of her marriage when Ken went away with the cattle for ten days at a stretch: 'She used to milk the goats – there was a terrible drought, so we weren't bothering to milk the cows then. There was no electricity, only fat lamps for the blacks and kerosene and lanterns inside the house . . . a great change after Sydney, but I always wanted to live on a station. I just loved it.'

Her baby grandson was also being looked after by an Aboriginal. 'I trust her completely and the child loves her.' Echoes of India and the ayah.

Vigilance is needed on such a homestead: a taipan, the worst of the local snakes, had been found in the house a few days earlier.

'What chance would you have, if bitten?'

'Nil,' said Ken. 'Deadly brutes.'

'Well,' Bob corrected him laconically, 'if you were bitten on the finger, you might have a chance by biting it straight off.'

Those few days on the station had a self-contained tranquillity and a powerful sense of belonging. In several weeks' time a priest was driving up from Townsville to christen two little Aboriginal girls, Queenie and Joycey, and the baby – Shane James Atkinson. Every Atkinson is called James, after Ken's grandfather. This would be a christening of the fifth generation, a big occasion, with a bush wedding nearby and the picnic races at Mount Garnet. For me the homestead represented the romance of Australia. As if to confirm this, one of the Atkinson sons handed me a scrap of paper with evident bashfulness when I left, and I was startled to discover that this silent man wrote poetry. Reading the first two verses today, every line is heartfelt and evokes that splendid scene:

> No dearer place could I desire than this
> To watch at sunset fire,
> The tired stock horses, one by one
> First rolling in the cool white sand
> Remove the mark of girth and band
> And then feed out towards the sinking sun.
> No sweeter music I could seek
> Than horse bells ringing down the creek.
>
> No velvet lawns of some older land
> Can hold me like that trampled sand;
> No garden wealth can thrill me through
> As these burnt broken wattles do,
> For there upon those Australian plains
> They all but hold my heart in chains.

Mile-high Witness

Arriving in Sydney from Hobart more than twenty-five years later, I found the city un-
recognisable: Americanised, divided into cliques. Happy in anticipation, I expected to
love it like everyone who goes there today, yet, in spite of the exhilarating harbour and
the generosity of my hosts, I experienced the *malaise* of loneliness in a crowd.

Without the *raison d'être* of the Merchant Navy or my television series, there was
little purpose to my stay, unless it was enjoyment, and I am one of the few who prefer
the sprawling suburb of Melbourne. Everyone looked so perfect in Sydney that they
might have been kept in aspic, while I was on the outside looking in.

I was the wrong age to appreciate the new brashness of the city, and thought wistfully
of the invitation in Tasmania to sail down the Arthur River and continue on safari to the
ghost town of Balfour. The only journeys I regret are those I failed to make.

I boarded my plane for the return flight with bemused regret that I had not enjoyed
myself more, yet content to know that I was going home. My seat was in the front row of
the business-class section which was half-empty, so I was able to spread my books and
possessions over the seats. Consequently, I was somewhat vexed when a breathless,
belated passenger appeared as we were about to taxi off, waving a ticket for the seat
next to mine. With singular ill-grace, I started to remove my possessions. She was a
bubbly, nice, friendly woman, rather attractive, in her mid-thirties, though I feared she
was an obsessional talker determined to use the flight as a confessional. She had started
already – where was I going, what was my name? She was called Noeline. While she
waited for me to clear the seat, her eyes flicked to the solitary passenger on the other
side of the aisle, and rested there. I had noticed his film-star looks already. He was

highly-tanned with immaculate hair and a golden medallion resting on his hairy chest. I suspected that he reeked of after-shave and wore a hugely expensive watch and hand-made slip-on shoes. Noeline's eyes swung back to me, and back again.

'Please,' she insisted in a baby-doll voice, her hands fluttering in protest, 'you really mustn't go to such trouble when I can perfectly well sit over there.' With a swift swivel she turned to the handsome man. 'Would you object if I sat here instead?'

'Be my guest!' he smiled, revealing a set of perfect teeth.

'Oh, thank you,' she beamed, and her eyes dilated.

It was my turn to chip in. 'Are you sure you don't want to sit *here*?' I asked.

'Positive,' she snapped.

Everyone fastened their seat-belts with relief.

Over the next few hours as we flew over the Australian desert, I observed a courtship of unabashed lust. A computer could not have matched them more perfectly, and their mutual attraction was enhanced by the free champagne supplied so generously by Qantas.

At last the lights were dimmed. Their flirtation grew even more vigorous, with giggles, muffled laughter and calls for more 'fizz', but I dozed off. I woke suddenly, hardly aware that I had been asleep, to find the cabin moribund apart from the noise of the engines and a curious rustling opposite. Peering into the gloom, the shock was un-avoidable – it was the legendary mile-high club come true, not in the stand-up position of the cramped lavatory but laid, literally, across the two seats opposite where no one but myself could see them.

Strangled sobs, grunts, and muffled groans eliminated doubt. I closed my eyes and sat there rigidly, anxious not to be caught as a voyeur, and afraid that if I moved I might spoil their climax, though I believe they would have remained impervious to a crash-landing. After further cries there was an eerie silence and I dozed off again.

In the light of morning they sat beside each other like two strangers. He occupied him-self with his book, she looked about her with a broad smile until she discovered that one of her ear-rings was missing. The upheaval which ensued would have been excessive if she had lost her virginity instead, and that was most unlikely. Her seat was virtually dis-mantled, and then she insisted that the steward inspect the man's as well, in spite of the steward's evident surprise that an ear-ring should have travelled so far. Every posses-sion was shaken and searched as the man – looking less tanned by the minute – was made to stand in the aisle. Even when the steward returned with a sort of hoover, naught was found.

'It's a mystery,' the steward exclaimed loudly.

'It most certainly is,' I agreed, in the voice of Oliver Hardy.

'You see,' she explained, 'it's the twin to this one.' She took off the remaining ear-ring and waved it ineffectually at the other passengers behind us, who were beginning to be amused. 'It hasn't any real worth, but it's sentimental – from a beau.'

Noeline was due to leave the plane at Karachi and she and the man did not exchange a word until we landed. With a gallantry that cost him considerable effort, he escorted her as far as the exit, kissed her formally on the cheek, and hurried back to his seat.

Anxious to stretch my legs, I found myself behind Noeline in the queue in the airport.

'Apart from the ear-ring,' I said with a smile, 'did you enjoy the flight?'

She looked startled for a moment, until she remembered that I had been sitting across the aisle, the only passenger to have witnessed everything.

'The flight?' she echoed, with such a radiant expression that I warmed to her at last. 'The flight. It was just *fantastic!*'

Tasmania – More English than England?

When I flew to Tasmania in 1961 I warmed to Hobart, the early settlement clustered round a fine natural harbour like a miniature Sydney, overshadowed by the mauve summit of Mount Wellington: 'Just enough of a mountain,' wrote Anthony Trollope, 'to give excitement to ladies and gentlemen in middle life.' I am not entirely sure what he meant – the ascent, presumably? – and have never agreed with his dictum that 'everything in Tasmania is more English than is England herself.' The light is completely different, so vivid that it picks out the emerald green hills in the distance, and bounces off the white weather-board homes and churches. The names are nostalgic – Launceston, Sheffield, New Norfolk, even Gretna Green – but they are belied by the immensity of their surroundings, by the massive gum trees and dense forests.

An island of startling variety, combining snow mountains and the shimmer of the Mediterranean, Tasmania is roughly the same size as Scotland. With a population of less than half a million there is a welcome absence of traffic and noise. After England and Turkey, Tasmania is my favourite country in the world. To think of it as a separate country is irresistible. On my last visit, after an interminable wait for my visa, the girl asked if I intended to leave Australia during my stay.

'I assume that Tasmania is part of it?' I asked.

'Only *just*!' she replied.

Ignored by the rest of the world, often left off the map of Australasia, in 1961 it felt as if Tasmania was suspended in limbo. We filmed a programme on the scallop fishermen and I stayed with a friendly family who fed me fried scallops for breakfast, scallops mornay for lunch, curried scallops for dinner – a treat for me, if not for them. When I sailed out with the boats I ate them fresh from the sea with the red sauce from the coral, better than oysters. I have not been able to face a frozen scallop since.

Though this was agreeable visually, it was heavy-going and I tried to find a more interesting subject on my return to Hobart.

'Take me to the one place I shouldn't go,' I told the taxi-driver, as I had often done before.

'No problem there!' he laughed. He stopped at a far corner of the docks and pointed to a pub at the end: 'No cab'll take you closer than this.'

It sounded promising, and sure enough Ma Dwyer's proved the toughest pub in town, a refuge for foreign sailors with a brothel upstairs run by Ma who had the proverbial heart of gold, though she seemed in a state of constant rage. Over the next few days, the

appearance of her customers changed drastically due to their scars from the drunken brawls, but the place mesmerised me for it took me back to the past. This was the other reason for the sense of limbo.

Tasmania, so tranquil on the outside, has one of the bloodiest histories on earth. In a matter of decades, the British wiped out a population which had survived for tens of thousands of years. No Aboriginal was left, apart from an unfortunate old woman who became a museum piece, and many of the indigenous animals were exterminated. , Little wonder that the Tasmanians were ashamed of their past. In 1961 they were so reluctant to talk about their convict ancestry that, when an American scholar arrived to do research into their background, he was persuaded to leave the island.

In less than five years, from 1841 to 1845, as many as 15,546 male convicts were transported to Van Diemen's Land, as it was known; 1,605 were sent to New South Wales. Altogether, more than 50,000 male and 10,000 female were subjected to conditions worse than those on Devil's Island. With a hideous irony, the worst cruelty was the most refined; in the model prison in Port Arthur the solitary cells had several doors to keep out the light, and the warders wore carpet slippers to ensure absolute silence. On the rare occasions when the convicts were allowed to go to church, those from the model prison wore calico masks with slits for their eyes. It is not surprising that a lunatic asylum was built nearby.

The luckier convicts were assigned as servants, others to the hard labour of the chaingang, building roads. If they defied authority, they were sent to the penal settlements. Macquarie Harbour was the first, founded in 1822 on the wild west coast, cast in everlasting cloud, with violent storms from the Antarctic in the winter, and rain for 300 days in the year. The conditions were so appalling that this remote and unpractical settlement was abandoned after ten years and replaced by Port Arthur on the west coast.

I knew none of this until I met Miss Carrie James. I heard of this remarkable woman from a local freelance journalist, Jack Millar, who told me she was ninety-four, kept alive by the responsibility of looking after her retarded nephew who was seventy and in danger of being committed to an asylum unless she vouched for him. Though she lived precariously in the present, Millar claimed that her recall of Hobart as a convict town was extraordinary.

We called at her sloping house in Upper Bathurst Street, made from the timbers of H.M.S. *Anson* which sailed on her last voyage from Portsmouth in 1843 with 500 male convicts, but Miss James either did not hear us or refused to open the door. After two more attempts, I abandoned hope, and Rollo decided to move to Melbourne and cover a football match which had been 'set up' in advance.

During a last, subdued dinner in the Wrest Point Hotel, Millar arrived in a state of agitation. Miss James was prepared to see me, though it was now too late to film her.

An hour later I was back in the hotel describing the extraordinary encounter. I spoke without guile, assuming there was no chance of changing our plans, but Rollo bemoaned the lost opportunity and Bob Wealthy murmured that it *might* be possible to change our tickets . . .

That was all Rollo needed. He insisted on seeing Miss James himself, but after five minutes he was convinced and we withdrew to let her rest until we returned in the morning.

In the light of day, I was less enthusiastic. The other story had been cancelled, to the fury of the camera crew, who were bored with Hobart and were looking forward to the football match. An interview with an old woman on the verge of dementia seemed a poor alternative, and I did not have the courage to warn them that she might refuse to open the door or prove too weak after our visits the previous evening.

We knocked repeatedly, hearing scuffling inside, but, as we turned away, the door opened and Miss James welcomed us inside. As scrawny as a shag, her eyes were neither pale nor watery but fierce in their intensity as she returned to the convict past with startling clarity. She remembered the female convicts who had been set free standing behind their garden gates, arms akimbo as they smoked their clay pipes and spat at the few passing settlers: 'They hated the migrants, they hated everyone – a hate in their hearts.'

Though she was born in Hobart, her parents were migrants. Her mother's family had sailed to Tasmania , and her father was so much in love that he followed and they married in Hobart. This sounded romantic, until Miss James described her loveless childhood: 'Father read the Bible and mother held the cane. Mother was cruel, "If you can't break their spirits," she said, "break their backs." But you break the spirit of a child and you ruin it for life. Sad old days and I shouldn't have lived among it . . .' She broke off dramatically, and cried out in anguish, cutting the air with her skeletal hand. 'Oh, don't they ruin a life. Never a cuddle, never a kiss.'

Carrie James remembered two convicts with affection. 'There was Charles, tall man, he got subservient, you know, but mother wouldn't have that . . . His spirit was broken, he left a comfortable home and loving mother, you see. He said, "I wish I had never been born." How could they be happy? I never saw one happy one. Homesick and broken spirited.'

Both Charles and Dick Stanton, the other convict she remembered with particular fondness, were deported on the most pathetic of charges. 'Charley was going along in London, only a boy of nineteen, when an old man with a barrow full of stuff said, "Give us a lift, lad," and of course he did – one of the softy sort – and the man ran away and the police found the boy with the barrow which was stolen.' She paused again, as her mind wandered: 'I think they all wished they were dead, but you know, life is *sweet* . . .

Stanton's crime sounded even less heinous. Miss James gave me some notes which he dictated to her father, starting with the flourish: 'Richard Stanton – of Her Majesty's Navy, at your service.' After reading *Robinson Crusoe* at the age of eleven, he developed 'an uncontrollable desire to follow a seafaring life' and in due course joined the Royal Navy in Portsmouth:

> After service of twenty months an event happened that altogether altered the course of my life's career. Her Majesty, Queen Victoria, who had been

Queen of Great Britain for some seven years, paid an official visit to the Fleet. The exciting news spread throughout our ship that the young Queen was to come aboard on the morrow.

I very much question whether any other event could have imposed more strenuous duty upon us all: standing gear had to be overhauled, the decks, always as white as holy-stone could make them, had to have an extra scouring, and the brasswork of which there was a warship's profusion, came in for exceptional burnishing.

For Dick Stanton, the visit meant disaster. As the royal vessel approached, some halyards came loose and he sprang to catch them:

> in my descent I cannonaded against a midshipman, a mere boy much my junior. He rolled down from the poop to the main deck, a distance of about three feet. He got up absolutely unhurt but in a fit of frenzy accused me of deliberately assaulting him, and no expostulation on my part was of any avail.

Miss James told me that she often wondered if Stanton had collided with the midshipman on purpose. The incident might have passed with reprimand and ordinary punishment, but Stanton had marred the special occasion. He ended his account with the touching comment: 'I was put under guard and so I missed the great delight I had anticipated of manning the yards to welcome Her Majesty.'

'Of course they needed men in Tasmania those days,' said Miss James, explaining the unusual sentence of deportation to Van Dieman's Land for two years. Leaving a grief-stricken family, he sailed in the convict barque *Argyle*:

> On one bright day the look-out reported, 'Sail ahoy to starboard!' and away in the distance were five ships of the line homeward bound from the Cape. To my experienced eye, how stately they were and I felt the hot tears coursing down my cheeks and I thought of the homeland I had been wrenched from. The chief officer saw my emotion and asked what offence I had committed. I said, 'None at all.' 'Ah,' he said, 'you all say that.'

Landing in Van Diemen's Land, Dick Stanton was assigned to a Major for household duties. 'The first day after my arrival I was given two large baskets of ladies' underclothing to wash and iron. I looked in astonishment, I remarked I would not disgrace the flag I sailed under, and danced "Jack's the lad with a hornpipe" on them.' This impertinence cost him twenty-five lashes. Miss James told me that once the convicts were assigned as servants, their masters could have them flogged as they pleased.

Flagellation was part of the existence endured in the penal settlement of Port Arthur, where Dick was sent for further punishment and subsequent flogging from Sam Burroughs – 'the flagellator' – Miss James spat out the words. 'We *hated* him. Quiet, the whole street was quiet when he came to Hobart, we all got on our doorsteps and watched the man go by with our little eyes . . . Dick would only show his back to our boys, the convicts didn't like the girls to look, but I thought, "I'll see that back," and one day I crept up and I did. Oh, *shocking*!' Her hand sketched the cuts on his back: 'Like a piece of leather, scored, scored, great weals, cross to cross.'

As Carrie James populated the past with stories of other convicts, I was able to picture Hobart a century earlier: a town where settlers, clergy and army officers were the exception, and convicts or freed men and women were the norm.

There was Mrs Rusk with one eye: 'She was a lady, you could tell – educated: why she was sent out I don't know,' – and 'poor' Mrs Buff, a lawyer's wife.

'Why poor Mrs Buff?' The question produced a succession of *non sequiturs*.

'Mrs Buff?' She gave me a look of surprise: 'Never knew. She was a very quiet woman. Lived on potatoes. She was burnt to death. She was starving; there was no pension those days, and the worms crept about her arms like this – ' She gave a graphic gesture, brushing them off. 'And she used to cut off wisps of her hair and eat them because she was told that would kill the worms. She used to come here and mother gave her food and was very kind to her, and put her in a rocking chair. She used to do a bit of washing around the place, but I bet she wasn't fit to do washing.'

'How did the burning take place?'

'Her clothes caught alight. She ran out of this awful little room at the back of the public house – you should have seen the flames – if they'd only made her lie down, but they were bashing her with bags . . . she didn't live long.'

'Did your mother have any convict servants?'

'Only one, Esther; she was eaten up with disease, poor thing.'

This was the background of Carrie's childhood: a boy of seventeen being marched down Macquarie Street to be hanged; screams in the night and murder; tough waterfront bars where seamen came in from the whaling fleets, echoed by Ma Dwyer's at the present time. Yet her humour was undefeated and she burst into cackling laughter when I asked if she regretted not having a family of her own: 'I had opportunities, but I couldn't click, somehow. No sex-appeal! My sister, oh, she had heaps of boys. I had a boy for a day or two, but he got sick of me. I was never meant to get married; I'm waiting for my spiritual mate.'

'Do you think love is the most important thing in life?'

'Yes, love is all, more than religion, love *is* all, love is all. I'm ninety-four and I know. It's not in what man possesseth, no, it's the heart; keep the heart with all diligence, for out of it are the issues of life.'

Far from being dismayed by our invasion of her house, with all the paraphernalia of the camera crew and lights, the experience seemed to revive her.

As the crew lugged their equipment into the street, each of them took me aside to congratulate me on the interview and to say how right Rollo and I had been to stay on. Miss James came to her door and I kissed her as we said goodbye. She waved after me and I ran down the hill to the nearest pub where I intended to get gloriously drunk on my own, knowing instinctively, that I'd just completed the most remarkable television interview of my career.

The following day we drove through splendid, wooded scenery to the former penal settlement of Port Arthur on the Tasman Peninsula. The infamous Eagle Hawk Neck is little more than a sandbar connected to the mainland, which used to be guarded by savage dogs chained every few yards to posts in the sand and even to platforms in the water on either side. On the rare occasions when they were fed, some of the meat was thrown into the water for the sharks, and one particular predator known as Government Billy. Any convict trying to escape had to risk attack from the dogs or the sharks. Few succeeded.

The ruins of the penal settlement sloped down to the water's edge, where the boats arrived from Hobart. Once the third largest town in the colony, a self-contained community with a church and hospital, a village green and parade ground, officers' bungalows and vast prison blocks, the prettiness of the shaded avenues and trim flower beds mocked the reason for Port Arthur's harsh existence. Even the home of the commandant, Captain O'Hara Booth – 'the personification of unimpassioned severity' – resembled a country cottage, with a jolly garden of fuchsias, roses, lupins and wide-eyed pansies. It was years before I discovered the full inhumanity of the model prison, which 'carried the vengeance of the law to the utmost limits of human endurance', but it seemed as if the anguish of the convicts had stamped a melancholy imprint on the ruins. Afterwards, as Rollo and I plunged into the icy surf of a lonely beach nearby, I looked at the overwhelming virgin forest which ran to the edge of the shore and wondered if the convicts were able to forgive this tremendous landscape, glimpsed on their working parties away from the settlement, laying tracks, felling timber.

In 1961 the past was unmentionable. The only literature in Port Arthur was a two-page leaflet which had the audacity to pretend that children had been sent to Point Puer 'for their own good', to flourish in the clean, fresh air denied them back home in the iniquitous back streets of the East End. Two of the boys had joined hands and jumped from the cliffs to their death on the rocks below, but such incidents had been erased, just as the names of convicts scratched on the walls of Richmond prison had been removed surreptitiously by descendants ashamed of the connection.

Back in England, the secret past of Tasmania began to obsess me. Carrie James wrote that she kept the flowers I had brought her, though they must have been brittle, enclosing an excruciating pair of pink bedsocks which she had knitted herself, so tiny that I gave them to a child. Soon afterwards, I heard from Jack Millar that Miss Carrie James was dead.

In London I discovered a lighter side to transportation. An old copy of the *London Literary Gazette* for 1822 described the arrival of a convict ship in Hobart, revealing that 'connexions spring up unexpectedly between the female convicts and *pretended* relatives by whom they are recognised, as it were, on their landing.' Research showed that female convicts were granted their freedom if they were claimed by a relative when they docked, and I imagined them enlisting the artifice of curling-tongs and the crimson dye from the bindings of Bibles, before their arrival, then swaying down the gangplank, like chorus girls descending a stairway with all the promise they could muster, as the sex-starved men rushed forward to greet them. In a land where women were outnumbered ten to one, they eagerly embraced the more attractive 'wives', 'sisters', and even 'aunts', whispering their real names as they did so. After the formalities had been completed or winked at, the younger women departed for a new life as free women, while the less fortunate were sent to a bleak reception hall. There they were likely to be raped by the soldiers who guarded them, a practice tolerated by the authorities. Like the boys in Point Puer, many of the women preferred to take their own lives.

My obsession with Tasmania's past led to an historical novel. The original title, *Convict*, was changed to the blander *Swansdowne* by the publishers, who feared the Australians might be upset by their reference to the past, unaware that attitudes were changing with the approach of the bicentennial celebrations.

In my foreword to the novel, I mentioned that Miss Carrie James had been the 'inspiration', and it seemed only fitting that I should name my hero, Dick, after the young convict whom she had remembered with such affection: 'Richard Stanton – of Her Majesty's Navy – at your service.'

Tasmania Revisited

Returning in 1987, I found the Tasmanians freed from lethargy and guilt, while Tasmania, unexpectedly, was even more beautiful than before.

I took the *Abel Tasman* ferry from Melbourne – the only passenger ship to operate in this part of the world – at six in the evening. After a merry voyage I woke to the heavy throb of engines – matched by my head – and scrambled on deck. We had just arrived at Devonport where two representatives of the Tasmanian Tourist Board were waiting for me: one was plainly efficient, brusque, suited and briefcased; the other reminded me of Crocodile Dundee – he wore a broad grin, a stockman's hat, mole-skin trousers and high-heeled boots.

I gathered that one would be my companion over the next few days and tried to hide my relief when the efficient man explained that he was needed in the office.

Darryl Stafford was a truckie for twenty years, and judging by his looks he must have started young. Trucking was his life. At competitions, he was a champion, winning awards for his skill in stripping and reassembling engines, maintaining his trucks with the devotion that a trainer might lavish on a horse.

Transporting massive logs from Tasmania to the mainland kept him away from home for most of the year. Finally his wife could bear it no longer and burst out: 'Tell me, Darryl, who do you love the most – the truck or me?'

He warned her angrily: 'Never ask me that again, or you'll hear something you won't like.'

When Darryl realised he would have to choose between his wife and his truck, it was as if the truck sensed that 'she' might be the loser and tried to kill him. Crossing a bridge, it veered out of control and plunged sixty feet into the Dove River below. If the trailer had been loaded, the logs would have crashed through the cabin killing Darryl outright. I would have struggled to escape through the window, but Darryl instinctively wound it up during those crucial seconds as the logs fell, knowing that the pressure would be too strong. As the truck settled on the riverbed, water poured through every crack until it reached his neck, but by then the outside pressure had eased and he managed to unwind the window, take a deep breath, and force his way through.

With the river in full flood, the torrent would have swept him away if he had not caught hold of the aerial on the roof, and, after taking another deep breath above the surface, he dived below, seizing everything he could clutch as he climbed along the truck until he reached the end of the trailer which rested near the riverbank.

'And then you collapsed?'

'No, I was fine. I realised I was safe and they didn't need me up above that day. But three months later I returned to that bridge, to the scene of the crime, as it were, and, as I walked across, I keeled over, and three months after that the nightmares started.'

His truck was salvaged but their love affair could never be the same again.

Darryl came home one evening a year later and told his wife he had packed in trucking for good. Nowadays, he drives a coachful of Tasmanians to Darwin on an annual tour in June, and she goes with him as cook. The coach has shown no jealousy – so far.

Darryl and his wife Joan lived with their two daughters, a dog called Fred and a piglet, Gussie, in a white, weather-boarded house 107 years old, which is historic by Tasmanian standards. It was plain that Darryl was now a contented man, a New Tasmanian who had come to terms with the past. He spoke of his Aboriginal great-grandmother with pride and recalled his grandparents' devotion: when her husband died, his grandmother sat motionless in her armchair and died herself seven days later. His Aboriginal ancestry entitles him to special rights - modern Tasmania's equivalent of guilt-money – which he does not claim.

I had returned to Tasmania to research my sequel to *Swansdowne* and on a fine spring day in early November we set off for Cradle Mountain, the singular, dipping mountain range featured on the cover. We drove past gleaming white wooden houses which resembled the colonial homes in a painting by Grandma Moses, and came to Boat Harbour, a small bay where the sand was so fine that it squeaked underfoot. The café on the edge of the shore offered a startling range of seafood, including a shrimp bisque and scallops and calamari in filo pastry.

'Darling, you've come to the best place in Tasmania and I'm the best hostess!' cried Mary O'Garey, a blonde with a mass of curls. As I ate a trevally fish caught in the harbour that morning, and tasted the Pipers Brook Chardonnay offered by two girls at the next table, I decided she had a point. I visited the Pipers Brook vineyard two days later. Perched on a hilltop with views over the Bass Straits and Mt Arthur to the north and a hundred miles of forest to the south, it must be the most spectacular winery in the world. Because the climate is colder than that of the Australian mainland, Tasmania is particularly suitable for high quality wine. The shrivelled grapes at the summit, exposed to the merciless wind, produced the finest taste of all.

That first afternoon after lunch we drove inland. The rolling landscape was so empty, apart from occasional sheep and cattle, that I might have stepped back a century. Then we climbed through forests of tall gum trees, interspersed with the twisted silver trunks of dead trees. The gums live for two hundred years, as opposed to the three or four thousand of the Huon pines in the rain forests, but when they die the roots rot and the trunks fall in the wind like rotten apples.

Cradle Mountain Lodge was surrounded by peaks still capped with snow. When it was dark, the lights were turned on outside and the wild animals arrived to eat in the protection of the National Park. I was enchanted by the possums and wild cats, less so by the tame wombat called Errol, after Flynn, who was born in Tasmania, which nipped me playfully but painfully on the ankle.

After midnight, Simon Current, the Englishman who spent a million dollars on the lodge, left for his own hut nearby while a few of us emptied a bottle of brandy beside a log fire and talked, as one can on such occasions, of nature and solitude and the joy to be gained from the animals.

I asked if the Tasmanian tiger was extinct, as people claimed, and one of the men told me that he had been clearing the bush with a bulldozer and fell asleep after lunch, waking some time later to see a striped tigress and her cub staring at him. The indigenous tiger, a sort of striped wolf, walked backwards a few yards and trotted away. 'Very shy,' he told me, 'you'd have more fear of the Devil than the tiger.' I thought this nice and biblical until I realised he meant the Tasmanian Devil which raided chickens and lambs and attacked wounded men, yet was able to survive, unlike the tiger which was allegedly shot to extinction. This man had seen the last known specimen in Hobart Zoo as long ago as 1926 or '7: 'The saddest creature I've ever seen. They don't live in captivity, they fret and die. Came out once a day, looked so miserable I thought if I ever saw one, I wouldn't tell. I'd let the poor bugger go, and I'd tell no man where I saw this tiger in the northeast. I haven't killed a snake for thirty years and I don't intend to. It's yer territory, I say, and walk round and they settle down.'

If this man was telling the truth, and there was no reason to disbelieve him, there is hope that the tiger may not be extinct after all.

The following morning, Darryl and I walked around Dove Lake at the foot of Cradle Mountain, crisp and alpine, and he showed me the chalet built from King Billy pine by Gustav Weindorfer, who lived there from 1911 until his death in 1932, his body discovered three days later beside his old bicycle. Understandably, Weindorfer has captured the imagination, and a memorial service is held in his honour each year with wild flowers placed on his grave, candles lit, and the recital of the poem starting: 'Into the wild wood he came . . .'. The last entry in his visitor's book reads: 'He died within sight of the mountains he loved and we have laid him to rest in the bosom of the valley with the sound of the murmuring pine and the singing stream.'

The bearded Austrian's life began promisingly in Vienna where he attended the University and became a linguist, geologist, architect and, above all, a naturalist, which is why he cut himself off from his fellow man on this remote corner of the world, literally a wilderness then, officially designated as such today. Surrounded by gum, myrtle, tea trees, blackwood and pencil pine, he built his chalet himself, apart from two weeks when he used a 'splitter' to make the necessary planks. It was big enough to hold as many as twenty people, but he preferred the company of his dog and the animals, as an entry in his diary for 1918 records:

> When the ground is all covered with snow, I do build a big fire, open my door, seat myself very, very quietly in front of the blazing logs and presently they come in one by one, the wild animals without their usual fear of man or one another, and share with me in stillness the grateful warmth.

It is obvious that he enjoyed his solitude, but it cannot be said that he lived alone.

Parting from Darryl in Launceston where I stayed the night, I caught the afternoon bus to Hobart which is one of my favourite towns. As Dublin used to be, it is just the right size, allowing one to explore on foot instead of in a vehicle. Nowadays the Tasmanians are rightly proud of their colonial buildings, flood-lighting the Town Hall and Customs House which were built in an earlier and more attractive style than their counterparts in Melbourne, which could be described as 'Scunthorpe Gothic'.

Sacrilege continues with highways on the waterfront at Sullivans Cove, but there is growing awareness that the island will benefit in the long run if the colonial architecture is preserved. Indeed, it is becoming a tourist attraction already in the case of Richmond, which boasts the graceful bridge built by the convicts in 1823, and the goal built *for* them a few years later, made from the honey-coloured local sandstone which features throughout the state. The goal has been restored and is open to the public, there are re-plicas of old shops which are nicely re-created, and this is the point. When the restoration is successful, as it is with Sovereign Hill north of Melbourne, it would be churlish to begrudge the effort, however twee, especially as the alternative would be neglect and ruin.

Never expect too much from travel. Rather than pursuing it, let the experience come to you. Though the rewards may seem infinitesimal to others, they can be infinitely gratifying to yourself. I was surprised by the way I adapted to Tasmania, shedding skins, finding new aspects of myself which my friends would have failed to recognise. Due to the sympathy of the place, I was content.

Apart from the flash casino in the Wrest Point Hotel, the first in Australasia, there are few bright lights in Hobart where the streets are quiet after six. I relished the absence of traffic as I walked past the warehouses of Salamanca Place to Battery Point, named after the battery of guns which protected the harbour, and the signal station erected as early as 1818 where the arrival of ships as they entered the Derwent River twenty miles away was relayed by signal from the top of Mount Nelson. The signal system was so effective that, if a convict succeeded in escaping from the hell-hole of Port Arthur, the message reached Hobart in minutes.

Battery Point has an unpretentious charm which saves it from becoming a museum piece, though it houses the Van Diemen's Folk Museum in addition to the old stone cottages and modest crescents like Arthur's Circus owned by Governor Arthur who sold the lots at auction in 1847. There was much to absorb: the splendid church of St George; the imposing entrance to Anglesea Barracks, confirming the taste as well as the fortitude of the early settlers recalled by Carrie James. Also, the unexpected bonus of restaurants such as Mure's Fish House, built in 1849 and owned today by a former Lowestoft trawlerman and his wife, where I feasted on local oysters, scallops and fresh crayfish; or Dirty Dick's which fed me huge, tender steaks.

I had been startled in Launceston to find that the front doors of restaurants were closed, so I had to knock to get in, and assumed this was protection against unwelcome visitors, curious in a country where people seldom lock their doors or even their cars. In fact it is a courtesy, welcoming the customers as if they are friends entering a private home, an impression enhanced by the dining-room furniture, carpets and pictures.

I was dining one evening in Dirty Dick's when I noticed an elegant woman across the room, eating on her own as I was, and I went across to ask if she would join me for a liqueur after she had finished her meal.

'Certainly not!' she exclaimed. 'I shall join you *now*.'

As we were occupying separate tables, this seemed the proper thing to do, and it proved an instantaneous rapport, like in a Hollywood comedy: Gable and Lombard, Cary Grant and Ingrid Bergman, and *she* at least lived up to that comparison. She had received rough treatment in the courts that afternoon, representing a mother who was fighting for custody of her child. Traumatically, she had a similar problem of her own, so she was glad to relax, and confide.

Intending to include a vineyard in my sequel to *Swansdowne*, I was spellbound by her account of the winery she had started with her ex-husband in North Queensland, and their dismay when the first planting failed and they discovered they had buried the cuttings upside down. Good material, I thought. We talked intimately till long past midnight when we were joined by the owner, Ted, a former policeman in England, and continued until it was light when she caught her plane to the mainland and I walked back to my hotel brimming over with foolish pleasure from this brief encounter.

However, it was time to start my research and I drove to Port Arthur. If proof was needed of change, I found it here. Not visible change, though the ruins of the penal settlement appeared less grim, but a change in attitude. Today Port Arthur is a tourist attraction, the past no longer obliterated but prettified with a Supper Show at the Broad Arrow Café with the silent film of Marcus Clarke's classic, *For the Term of His Natural Life* 'in the authentic atmosphere – right where it all happened!'; and a cruise to the Isle of the Dead where convicts were dumped without water as punishment. Charabancs disgorged the visitors who wandered chuckling through the museum at the implements which were used for torture.

The next day I was driven to New Norfolk and beyond in search of the landscape I had created for *Swansdowne* on the basis of a few old documents and photographs. My companion was Kaye Hosking, who sensed exactly what I was hoping to find.

In the early days people caught a boat or coracle and travelled downstream with the tide and swirling currents to Hobart Town; the outward journey had to be made by horseback, but now there were roads and Kaye drove me inland through a landscape which grew increasingly familiar although I had never seen it before.

'One thing wrong,' I suggested. 'The trees should be denser.'

'They were,' she laughed, 'a hundred years ago, when you wrote about them.'

Onwards to those evocative names – the Black Hills, Gretna and Rosegarland, Bothwell and Clyde Hill, which overlooked the Hamilton Plains and the village of Hamilton itself. This was the town I intended to 'invent' for my sequel – astonishing to find it in reality, much as I had imagined. In 1839 Hamilton had a population of 779, which included 300 convicts, the indispensable flagellator and eleven petty constables. There were several pubs with such disarming names as Tasmanian Lass, The Hit and Miss, and The Crooked Billet, whose landlord was the hangman. The schoolmaster earned £75 a year, while the bounty on the Tasmanian tiger was £1 per head, which helps to explain its extinction.

I spent the night in Emma's Cottage, built in 1830 and restored as a labour of love by Judy Madden, a warm-hearted woman whose welcome made me feel part of the family when I dined in the Maddens' house that evening.

The next morning her husband Mike drove me over the sloping fields to the Fat Doe River, renamed the Clyde, a tributary of the darker Derwent. This was where I had pictured the house called Swansdowne. The haze and pouring rain enhanced the odd sensation that I was entering the landscape of my imagination.

I walked towards the edge of a creek bordered by willows and fallen trees and there it was – a house across the water which could have been Swansdowne except that it was ruined. For one split-second I expected my characters to emerge from the ruins and greet me, yet knew that if they did I would have been a ghost myself.

This was not the end of that eerie, unforgettable day.

I visited Hamilton's singular church, built by the convict architect John Lee Archer. It was laid out as early as 1834, before the founding of Melbourne, and consecrated in 1938 by the Bishop of Calcutta who travelled especially to this remote part of his diocese. Built of the glowing sandstone taken from the quarry behind, the church has neither clock nor steeple, due to a lack of funds, and it has a single door to prevent any convict from escaping if brought to a service. The graveyard was overrun by blue iris and periwinkles planted by the early settlers. Fascinated by the tombstones, I found one marking the death of Sarah Lane in 1844 whose dress was set alight by the wood-stove at the back of the church:

> This little inoffensive child
> To Sunday School had trod
> But sad to tell, was burnt to death
> Within the house of God.

Another, for a girl of twenty, read:

> Weep not for Me, my Mother dear
> I ham not ded but Sleeping here
> My ned you no, my Grave you see
> Prepair your self to follow Mee.

My research in Tasmania was over, for I had found the setting for my new novel. I had already 'roughed-out' the climax, ending it at Gallipoli with the death of two half-brothers, one an English officer, the other an Australian Anzac soldier, killed in the same dug-out by the same shell. I was obsessed by that campaign. In Turkey I had gone especially to Gallipoli, swam at Heles, and looked down on Suvla Bay from Lone Pine Cemetery, hauntingly beautiful, lined with cypress and pine, wallflowers and snapdragons growing between the gravestones with their poignant inscriptions: 'Dear is the spot to me where my beloved son rests. My Anzac Hero, Mother.'

Now I entered that cool and pleasant church in Hamilton prompted by curiosity, and as a kind of courtesy. On the wall rested a solitary plaque:

> In Loving Memory of
> PTE William John Alder Brown
> No 683 14th Battn AIF – 28
> PTE Harold Baylie Brown
> No 1159 15th Battn AIF aged 22 years
> Both killed in action at Gallipoli Peninsula (Anzac) 2nd May 1915.

Two brothers killed on the same day in Gallipoli: was this beyond a ghostly coincidence? Obviously not; but it has prevented me from writing my sequel.

Respite in Turkey

Why do I love Turkey so much? The obvious answer lies in the country and the Turks themselves, who prove the opposite of every preconception, but there was something more: the luck of going there at the right moment.

My first visit scarcely counts, though it did have an element of escapade. It occurred in the early 1960s, when I was able to afford a car and even someone to drive it (after passing my test, I realised it could be disastrous if I drove myself and so I employed a driver – one of the wisest decisions I have made).

He was a splendid man who lived in one of the suburbs with his girl-friend, and I thought it would be a nice idea for the two of us to drive to Marseilles and catch a boat to Istanbul. This came about after I suggested a series on the First World War to the ITV company I was working for. Usually receptive to my ideas, they rejected this one with such scorn that I retaliated by asking for a six months' sabbatical in order to visit the war graves at Flanders, as I had intended. With either magnanimity or the wish to get rid of me, they agreed to this arrogant request and when I returned they had the generosity to admit that I had been right all along, having learnt that the BBC were proceeding with a similar project.

I set off with the satisfaction of believing this would give my driver the experience of a lifetime. Beware of such condescension, however good the intentions. No good deed should ever go unpunished, and nor was this.

From the moment we left Calais I realised my mistake. Like so many Englishmen, he distrusted 'abroad', detesting French food, French hygiene and the nasty way the French talked French. I boarded the ship at Marseilles with relief after he glared at a plate of *bouillabaisse* as if it had done him wrong.

When we reached Istanbul we found the city was under curfew due to a small revolution. Instead of the fun and exploration I had been looking forward to, I looked down glumly from my hotel window on gun-boats growling up a lifeless Bosphorus. So the next day we drove to Izmir in the rain, and the sun came out to greet us when we arrived. However, by now my driver was beginning to crack. The horrors of abroad – the fleas, Turkish food, my own intolerance – and a desperate ache to see his girl-friend back home brought this large, lovely man to the verge of a nervous breakdown. Before he was carted off to a Turkish hospital or attempted to kill me, I put him on the next flight to London.

Much as I sympathised with him, this meant that I was left with a Ford Zodiac I could not drive, the boot filled with Iznik tiles I had acquired on the way. An agency put the car on an Italian ship full of Germans bound for Piraeus. There I stepped on to the quay and asked the first taxi-driver who possessed a smattering of English to act as my chauffeur for the following week. When I had the luck to meet the writer Peter Mayne, several of us drove to a headland close to Athens for lunch every day, talking and laughing away the afternoons. I should have ventured further, but my abortive trip to Turkey had dulled my eagerness for exploration. As soon as I found an Englishwoman who was happy to drive the Zodiac back to England with her family, I flew back to London, where in due course, driver, car and myself were reunited.

My next journey took place in 1982 under very different circumstances. I had committed financial suicide by throwing up my job in television in order to retreat to Devon to find out if I could write, losing my car, my driver, and eventually my beloved house in North Devon in the process. Moving to a nearby village, I caused a furore by writing a humorous article for the *Evening News* magazine on the penalties of living in the country, with the perennial difficulty of finding fresh vegetables such as spinach. My humour may have been heavy-handed, but the intention was plain from the frieze of jolly cartoons. Someone in the village who must have disliked me exceedingly circulated copies of the offending article, without the cartoons, which caused an extraordinary stir, although I had praised the village unreservedly elsewhere and love it still. The climax came with a front-page attack in the local paper which quoted an 'angry' woman: 'If Daniel Farson was beside me now I'd wrap the fresh fruit and veg around his neck and throw him over the quay.' Turkey rescued me from these doldrums.

A friend who worked for Greek public relations offered me a free flight to Salonika, though he did his best to discourage me against continuing to Turkey, warning of robbery, physical attack and danger in general – my first experience of the hatred of the Greeks towards the Turks, though the man was English.

When I took the ferry to the island of Thassos two mornings later it was the first of May in every sense. Unlike most of the Greek islands, Thassos is lush, almost alpine, with meadows and pine forests, lizards scurrying into the grass, and the distant shapes of mountains blurred by smoky haze. I booked into the Timoleon, with a balcony which overlooked the jetty, and the next day I took a bus to Panayia, a simple hillside village. After a breakfast of honey and yoghurt in the square, I followed a path which led me down beside a jostling stream through glades of olives until I reached a curve of perfect white sand stretching for several miles. The sea was such a translucent green that I remember it still.

I rented a folding bicycle and caught the bus to Potamia. As the bus sped off, I discovered that a vital screw had fallen off. With an ingenuity which surprised me, I made a splint by breaking a piece of wire from a fence, and rode downhill on the shuddering machine which threatened to jack-knife at any moment, hurling me on to the tarmac.

After four days I caught an early ferry laden with planks and empty bee-hives to the mainland port of Keramoti, where I boarded a bus to Xanthi and changed there for yet another to Istanbul. By now, my batteries were recharged with confidence.

My first impression of this incomparable city may not have been as prosaic as Richard Hannay's in *Greenmantle*, who compared the minarets to 'factory chimneys', but it was subdued. I arrived in the dark and my taxi-driver had not heard of the Pera Palas, the most venerable hotel in Istanbul, built in 1892 for the first passengers to arrive on the Orient Express, who were carried from the station by sedan chair. My initial disappointment at finding a noisy crowd of jostling Japanese and garish posters on the marble columns in the foyer was dispelled by the graceful wrought-iron lift worked by an attendant in brocaded livery. In the splendid bar mirrors reflect the room decorated with tulip-tiles, and the immense Middle Hall is a baroque folly worthy of a Turkish palace, in brown, yellow and gold, the ceiling inset with domes and windows. Today this grand hotel has been restored to its full glory. When the tables are laden with food for a celebration and the orchestra plays you are swept back to the days when the Palas was patronised by Kemal Ataturk – his room is preserved upstairs. Mata Hari, Greta Garbo and Edward VIII were other guests, while Agatha Christie wrote much of *Murder on the Orient Express* in her bedroom. The Palas is owned by three trustees, one of whom is the great hotelier, Hasan Süzer, who distribute a substantial share of the profits to children's charities, so you have the added satisfaction of knowing that you are drinking your *raki* on behalf of the poor.

Waking in my massive bedroom with old-fashioned furniture, next door to Ataturk's, I was already infatuated with Istanbul. I strode down the hill, past the fish-market and across Galata Bridge lined with men who fish so patiently, and frequently *do* pull something out of the dirty waters of the Golden Horn. The street vendors harangue the passers-by hopefully, trying to sell rolls of sticky-tape or combs, making a living from just a few successes. I sensed their shared defiance which symbolises Turkey, their indomitable cheerfulness, the great roar of the city, and that enchanted skyline of domes and minarets emerging from the morning haze, taking shape as if in a water-colour. I was in the East. I returned eventually to the Pera Palas, footsore but blissful, to meet my guide.

'I am number one man in Istanbul,' Yusuf greeted me. 'Twenty per cent of Istanbul knows me. I do not know them. Funny! My mother was a countess, my father a count, I am son-of-a-gun.'

'You certainly are,' I agreed.

Wiry and swarthy, with the penetrating eyes of a police interrogator, Yusuf exuded intrigue like a character from a bad film about the Casbah, with myself as a sweaty Sydney Greenstreet following in the wake of his Peter Lorre. He claimed he had lost his voice escorting a party of Japanese on the recently re-opened Orient Express, but this was hard to believe, for he never stopped talking. For Yusuf, interruption was the spice of conversation.

This was the first time I had been granted the privilege of a guide and I began to realise how delicate the relationship can be. At first I regretted his company, too strident, too clever, overwhelming me with his superior knowledge, moving at a breathless pace according to his schedule, leaving me little chance to sit down and stare. Small boys who simply wished to look at my camera or practise their English were pushed away violently, and petty officials bullied. Then we developed a mutual, sardonic understanding, and a grudging respect as I began to appreciate that he knew the city backwards. And this came close to affection when he laid on a banquet in the Facyo restaurant on the Bosphorus, where he commanded an astonishingly varied meal to prove the range of Turkish seafood – giant prawns from Iskenderum in the south, turbot from the Black Sea . . . course after course. Outside Russian tankers loomed in the distance while jaunty tugs thrust through the choppy currents. Yusuf had discovered one of my weaknesses – gluttony – and as I sipped the excellent Doluca dry white wine, I looked on him more kindly.

Even so, he descended on places with such authority, indulging in a volley of shouts and shaken fists, that I began to wonder if he belonged to some secret society.

'How many people have you actually *killed*?' I asked at one exasperated moment.

'I prefer make crime,' he replied mysteriously. To show he was joking, he added, 'My wish is for the advancement of humankind and world culture.' He came up with many phrases like that.

Nothing was beyond his intelligence, no human experience denied him – or non-human for that matter. With uncharacteristic discretion, he suggested that he had been involved personally in some 'close encounter'. Had the visitors from outer space, I wondered, landed, listened to Yusuf and gone away?

Yet disconcertingly, his wildest claims proved to be true. Allegedly fluent in sixteen languages, I discovered that he had written a guide-book to Istanbul in Japanese. He looked slightly hurt at my surprise: 'You did not understand,' he rebuked me, 'that I am part-Japanese?'

It turned out that Yusuf was responsible for the colour photographs in the brochure of the Pera Palas, where he was well-known and moved with impunity. In the Middle Hall I had further proof of Yusuf's versatility as he sketched me on a piece of pink paper.

'I did not realise you were an artist, too.'

'My pictures are everywhere in Spain.'

'The Prado?'

'No,' he corrected me indignantly. 'All in private houses.' He signed the portrait with a flourish – El Turco – presumably the equivalent of El Greco. I have kept it ever since in case of vanity, for this would be dispelled by the rosebud lips of Oscar Wilde, the mirthless eyes of Edward Heath, and a look of horror all my own.

'Life-like,' I remarked wanly, with the awful suspicion that it was. Indeed I grow more like it every year.

'But of course,' he smiled, accepting the compliment. 'No problem!'

Yusuf never let me down, until my last evening when he did not appear. As I waited for him in the bar of the Pera Palas, I thought I was going to miss my plane to Antalya. Gradually I became aware of music from a distant room which grew so discordant that I paused mid-drink to listen – someone was playing the piano very badly. El Beethoven? It had to be, and was.

'You did not know I am musician?' Yusuf looked up proudly from the keyboard as I hurried in.

'No. But I recognised your touch.'

At the airport I sensed that Yusuf was bracing himself to ask me a question. He was in love with an English girl who had worked at the British Embassy in Ankara, and as she had not replied to his letters, he wondered if I could intercede on his behalf. Back in England, she did not reply to my letters either. Perhaps she realised that Yusuf was not transferable. My flight was called and as we said goodbye I was almost sad to see the last of Yusuf. Inevitably, I saw him again, in Pamukkale, where those freak calcium formations resemble a glacial fairyland of petrified falls and small lakes of different colours. I swam in the hot-water thermal pools outside my motel, apparently surrounded by ice and snow, and looked down on the vast dark plain of Denizli below.

Another motel has a pool strewn with Roman ruins, for this was formerly Hierapolis, founded by Eumanes II, King of Pergamum in 190 BC and adopted by the Romans as a spa. I was peering into the Sacred Pool when I heard a familiar voice from behind the oleanders. 'I wait for you,' said Yusuf reproachfully.

'But how . . . ?' Then I realised that our meeting was pure coincidence as he waved to the party of Japanese he had been escorting. The reason he had stayed behind became apparent when he took me on a tour of Hierapolis. We came to a bleak corner near the Temple of Apollo called Plutonium, after Pluto the lord of the underworld; beside an archway, there was a sign marked DANGER. Yusuf explained that inside there was an underground cave connected to the temple, which had a 'treasure-trove of gold and jewels'. He was preparing for his descent, dressed either in a space suit or in a diver's outfit, complete with his own oxygen.

'Oh yes?' I remarked sceptically.

'You do not understand,' he continued impatiently. 'It is poison inside, the air is sulphuric acid, so your lungs are burnt. That is why no one has found the treasure, until myself.'

It was then that I happened to look down and saw that the ground was dotted with

dead birds. 'You see!' Yusuf smiled triumphantly. 'The birds fly inside at night and are killed by the poison as they try to escape.'

I shook my head with admiration. 'You never cease to amaze me, Yusuf!' He smiled forgivingly.

There is nothing new under the sun. Some months later I learnt that Strabo witnessed the same phenomenon when he visited the Plutonium two thousand years ago. The Greek historian, born in 63 BC, described the entrance as large enough to admit a man and very deep, and if there was no wind a man could approach it safely:

> . . . but for any living creature which enters inside death is instantaneous. Bulls, for example, which are taken in, collapse and are brought out dead; we ourselves sent in small birds which at once fell lifeless. The eunuchs of Cybele, however, are immune to the extent that they can approach the orifice and look in, and even penetrate some distance, though not normally without holding their breath.

Nothing had changed – apart from the eunuchs – the corpses of the little birds lay before us in evidence. Yusuf had been vindicated once again.

My second guide to Turkey proved the perfect antidote to Yusuf. Ibrahim Buyukbenli met me at Antalya airport, advancing towards me with the waddle of a jovial penguin. He was a gentle man and told the story of his limp over dinner on the open, prow-like restaurant of the Talya, surely one of the most luxurious hotels in the Mediterranean.

Ibrahim had been thrown by a horse at the age of seven, badly injuring his foot. Money was scraped together to send him to Izmir, but a bulldog on the boat, alarmed by the upturned foot which seemed about to kick him, pursued the boy everywhere, snarling and biting, which hardly mattered except that Ibrahim loved dogs. This has been his penalty ever since, but it has not deterred him.

A few years ago he saw a stray dog sleeping in front of the wheels of a jeep and lifted the animal out of harm's way. In the panic of being woken, the dog scratched him. Ibrahim went to a doctor who warned him that unless he could trace the dog within the next four days and find it free from disease, he would have to undergo a course of injections. Ibrahim and his friends searched every corner of Antalya with increasing desperation, but the dog had vanished. Ibrahim started the injections and after the fourteenth his body became partly paralysed; another man died from the same treatment. Eventually Ibrahim recovered but had to convalesce for the next eight months.

On his first day back at work, thankful to be active once again, he saw the same stray dog trotting along the edge of the pavement, tail wagging and perfectly well. Ibrahim stared at the dog dismayed – his year of pain had been for nothing.

Ibrahim had found a receptive audience, for I love dogs myself and listened closely. Warming to his theme, he said, 'But I have happy story today.' A few months earlier someone had told him of an abandoned dog in a nearby village whose neck was horribly twisted by a coil of wire, probably used to tie it up as a puppy, which was now strangling the animal as it grew larger.

Ibrahim fetched the local vet, hired a car, and set out for the village, where everyone denied all knowledge of such a dog. Finally a boy followed the limping Ibrahim and whispered that he might find the dog in a ruined house on the outskirts. Sure enough, Ibrahim saw a flash of frightened eyes in a dark corner and, as the dog made a dash for the entrance, he managed to seize it by the ears – foolhardy in view of his previous experience. The vet moved in smartly and gave it an injection: together they cut the wire, cleaned up the abandoned dog, and when it recovered it was free. Before they left, Ibrahim gave some money to the boy to feed the dog, and if this sounds naïve I should add that the Turks are noted for their honesty. As for the vet, he refused his fee protesting, 'If you're mad enough to do all this for a strange dog, then I haven't got the heart to charge you.'

'Bravo!' I exclaimed, delighted.

Ibrahim leant forward, smiling: 'But here is the good news. This morning a man came to my office to tell me that the dog had just had five puppies and all are doing well.'

Over the next few days I discovered Ibrahim's sly sense of humour and unexpected passions. At one place I noticed an older man with an attractive younger woman and wondered about their relationship.

'Eighty-five!' Ibrahim whispered gleefully.

'What?' The man did not look that old.

'You look at her breasts.'

'Well, as a matter of fact . . .'

'I can always tell size of ladies' breasts. I am expert!' For a moment it might have been Yusuf.

We spent a week together travelling up the coast to Marmaris. Of all the places we visited, the mountain city of Termessos was the best.

I had not heard of Termessos, I had no idea what to expect. Like so many, I suffered from the misconception that Turkey is a barren country, so my first delight was the freshness of the air as the car climbed through pine trees for the last zig-zag miles. Wild roses and banks of yellow broom grew beside the gorge, and a determined tortoise crossed ahead of us.

After we stopped at a clearing we continued by foot, with Ibrahim scrambling up the path with startling agility for someone so lame. As so often in Turkey, there was the combination of gentleness and power: first the increasing delicacy of the wild flowers – wild orchid, familiar forget-me-nots and lady's slipper, until we reached the ramparts of the city. Suddenly the walls loomed above us, set in a fold of the mountain range near the peak of Güllük Dag which is also known as Mount Solymus, explaining why the Termessians frequently described themselves as Solymians in their inscriptions.

With my woeful ignorance of ancient civilisations, I was awestruck when Ibrahim explained that 45,000 people lived here until the earthquake in the fifth century scattered the ruins over the mountainside, where they remained undisturbed until they were discovered by a German archaeologist in 1885.

The idea of people choosing to live against the odds, and beating them, enthralls me, but what audacity induced the Termessians to live in such an eyrie? That, of course, was the strength of it. Termessos was impregnable. 'These hills,' wrote Arrian, 'form a kind of gate in the road so that a small defence force can easily render the passage impossible.'

At the same time the Termessians were notorious for swooping down from their lair to pillage the coastal ports, racing back to the mountains with their loot and any girl who caught their fancy. The people of Phaselis, in particular, had reason to hate the Termessians, and when Alexander the Great made his winter headquarters there in 333 BC, taking advantage of the three harbours, the Termessians were rash enough to raid the town while he was there. There have been suggestions, as Ibrahim explained, that it was really the people of Phaselis themselves who 'arranged' the attack, convincing Alexander that his honour had been insulted. If so, their ruse succeeded and Alexander rode into the horseshoe valley below Termessos where the hills formed the gate referred to by Arrian. The Termessians watched from the slopes above, poised to defend their city, but Alexander pitched his tents for the night believing that the Termessians would retire to their city overnight, leaving a token force which he could quickly overcome. And this is what happened, except that when Alexander approached the city the Termessians released gigantic nets filled with stones and boulders which created an avalanche, cascading on to the soldiers below, wounding Alexander's horse and killing several of his men. With the scornful excuse that he could not be bothered with a protracted siege of such an insignificant eagle's nest, he rode out of the horseshoe valley, though he set fire to their precious olive groves as he did so. Termessos, therefore, is unique; the one place in the world which Alexander the Great was unable to conquer.

The Grecian theatre at Termessos, which hangs on the mountain face 3,500 feet high like a great curved nest, is one of the most spectacular examples of man imposing himself on nature. With the tiers of seats which held an audience of 4, 500 remarkably intact, the fallen stones across the orchestra where the wild animals were released through five doors, the range of the Taurus mountains behind and great Pamphylian plain below me, this was one of the most exhilarating sights in my life.

Termessos had twenty temples, a shopping centre, and the customary gymnasium with hot baths where the athletes relaxed and washed off the oil and sand. Also, there were three vast underground containers the size of small houses, linked by stone steps and passages. Sometimes they are referred to prosaically as water cisterns, enabling the Termessians to withstand a protracted siege, but as there was a spring supplying constant fresh water I preferred Ibrahim's assurance that these were oil wells, even that the oil was channelled down to Antalya along the earliest 'pipelines' in the world.

All this was stupendous enough, but there was something more – the spirit of the city. *Polis* means city, so *acropolis* is the city on the hill, while *necropolis* is a city for the dead. Usually found on the outskirts, the necropolis formed the very heart of Termessos, as the remains of 10,000 tombs strewn among the trees and boulders prove. Many visitors are unaware of a second necropolis higher up which Ibrahim insisted on showing me, leading the way swiftly in spite of his upturned foot. The climb became strenuous as I followed over the rocks, suddenly freezing as a long grey snake slithered into the cracks of a tomb. Harmless, Ibrahim assured me, unless it bit me in the neck. The reward was finding the tombs much as the earthquake had left them, decorated with the shields which symbolised the courage of the Termessians, lions and gryphons, and the open-mouthed Medusa heads which warned potential grave robbers that they would be turned to stone themselves if they dared disturb the tombs, a warning disregarded by time.

The Termessians adopted the Roman practice of limiting grief to a definite period, using a tear-glass, like an eye-bath, into which they poured their stricken tears. When the glass phial was full, it was sealed with wax and placed beside the corpse as proof of his goodness when he stepped into the hereafter – 'Look how they wept for me!' If he was disliked or his family so indifferent that they found it hard to shed a tear, they resorted to the market, where professional weepers filled the phials for them.

Later, I visited the museum at Side to see examples of these tear-glasses and the tombs of two children. No fierce Medusa heads for them, for they had nothing worth stealing, but there were decorations of the sweetest poignancy: a dog peering wistfully around an open door; flowers, to show the child was mourned; a swallow, to indicate the family had moved away; a butterfly, to suggest the reincarnation they hoped for; a basket of cotton to last a lifetime, with only two notches on the bobbin to explain that the girl was two years old when she died. On the small, carved steps of the doorway lay the mother's bleeding heart.

Only the Medusa heads watched us from the undergrowth at Termessos that day; there were no souvenir shops, and no visitors apart from ourselves. No ruined city has equalled that first impression.

Ibrahim's guidance enhanced every moment. His knowledge was all the more remarkable for being self-taught. His education had come to an abrupt end with the fall from his horse and subsequent illness. When he was nineteen he worked for an American firm which was laying diesel pipelines across the country. He learnt English and became an English-speaking guide, though his lack of education kept him on a low grade with a salary of £60 a month, even on the verge of retirement when he was accepted as the doyen of guides.

Regarding a sympathetic rapport as crucial – 'People are like envelopes, until you open them up you cannot understand them' – he refused to be rushed – 'I am not robotic guide,' refusing to 'do' a ruined city in a slot fitted into a schedule.

When Prince Rainier and Princess Grace came to Antalya for a conference arranged by Jacques Cousteau on the dangers of pollution in the Mediterranean, all the first-rate guides were flown in especially from Istanbul and Ankara. They were unable to answer the questions of Princess Grace who was interested in early civilisations, so the lowly Ibrahim was called on instead.

'But I am only eighth-grade guide,' he protested, savouring every second of his power.

'That doesn't matter,' they told him impatiently. 'Today you can be first-grade, we need you.'

Princess Grace insisted on having Ibrahim as her personal guide for the rest of the visit. On her last evening, Ibrahim had not been invited to the official cocktail party because of protocol. She refused to start without him, so the exasperated officials had to rush to his home for the second time.

When he appeared, Princess Grace waved to him to join her and he waddled through the 500 guests to sit at the top table beside her. She kept him talking about mythology for an hour until Ibrahim felt the scorching glares of the dignitaries and made his excuses: 'Princess, you are very important person and I should not like to prevent others from seeing you. It is time I go back to my home.'

The next day, Prince Rainier presented Ibrahim with a medal and a family album of photographs, adding: 'If you should ever come to Monaco, I shall show you *my* country and *we* shall be your guide.'

Ibrahim in Monte Carlo was not an image that sprang easily to mind, though I savoured the fantasy at the castle gates, as he mopped his brow and wiped his spectacles before the guards turned him away. And then, as he limped down the hill, a cry from an upper window and a wave from the Princess in the best tradition of fairy tales as she called him back, remembering his wisdom and his courtesy.

This is how I felt towards him when we parted company at Marmaris. Through his gentle humour I had gained an insight into Turkey, and I embraced him suddenly on the quay, kissing him on both cheeks in the Turkish style. I had made a friend and I had found a country. Everyone should have a second country, if possible, and from that moment Turkey has been mine.

Bruised Fingers

'Do be careful,' warned a close friend in Ankara when she heard that I was travelling to the north-east of Turkey on my own.

'In what way should I be careful?' I asked, brightening at this hint of danger.

'Don't go out at night in towns like Kars, and if anyone stops you taking photographs, do not argue. Don't argue about anything.' She knew me well. 'If you find yourself in trouble, smile and apologise, explaining that you had no idea what you were doing.' She sighed anxiously. 'Yes Daniel, please be careful.'

This sounded promising. I took the train from Ankara to Erzurum, which my friend regarded as madness. No Turk travels by train. If they are too poor to fly they go by bus which cuts the time in half. By air that journey takes an hour and costs less than £15. My journey lasted twenty-nine hours and cost £6. From a logical viewpoint, such a form of travel is masochistic yet I rejoice in the sublime indifference of Turkish trains. There was no buffet or restaurant car, but I had a compartment to myself so it would have been difficult to run into trouble if I had wanted to. As my 'express' was three hours late in starting, I had time to buy barbecued chicken with rice from a stall near the station. When the train started to cross vast plains or wound its way through gorges beside a swirling, dirty-yellow river without a man-made obstacle in sight, I relaxed. In the morning, I woke to find a new terrain of immense dun fields and straw-coloured hills. This is why I travel by train: to savour the overwhelming size and emptiness, the realisation that Turkey is more a continent than a country, and the excitement of knowing that I am heading east.

First impressions can be a treacherous mix of dispiriting weather, wrong people, and hateful accommodation. Even the time of arrival is critical. As my taxi drove from the station in the rain in the middle of the afternoon, Erzurum confirmed its reputation as a rough, tough, forbidding town. Gradually, I understood that toughness is integral to the largest city in the east of Turkey.

Set in a vast plain, the area has been fought over for centuries as a vital link in the trade routes from Asia, linking Trebizond on the Black Sea with Doğubayazit near Persia and Lake Van to the south. Known to the Byzantines as Theodosiopolis in the fourth century, after the Emperor Theodosius, it represented the furthest frontier of the Eastern Roman Empire – Arz-er-Rum, 'the land of Rome', hence Erzurum. A series of invaders swept in from the east: Mongols, Turks, Seljuks, and finally the Russians, who held the town on three occasions. They withdrew after the First World War when Ataturk declared his Republic and concentrated on their own revolution. Erzurum today is still a military garrison, though a noted university too.

The weather is as forbidding as its history: the winter lasts for seven months, so harsh that many of the surrounding peasants live underground. It is followed by a brief summer of ferocious heat, although I enjoyed a welcome respite early in October. Undeniably, Erzurum is a sombre place, with men wearing cheap plastic clogs or toeless socks, women shuffling forward like walking sacks, their faces totally obscured. Yet, as so often when life is hard, there is an atmosphere of cheerful defiance from the shoeshine boys who pose ebulliently for photographs, and from the young Turks walking arm in arm, or three-in-arm, with a cosy comradeship that would earn them disapproving glares in Piccadilly. As always in Turkey, the smiling faces and laughter lessen the adversity.

After the severity of Erzurum the town of Artvin provides a startling contrast. Driving through increasingly mountainous scenery, skirting the perilous edges of the cliffs above Lake Tortum, you gain the impression of height but this is deceptive. In spite of the flatness of the plain, Erzurum is Turkey's highest provincial capital, at 6,400 ft above sea level it is known as 'the roof of the world'. The vegetation along the rivers that swirl through the gorges in the north confirms a more moderate climate and the approaching mildness of the Black Sea coast: a surprising mixture of fig, blackberry, pomegranate, even tamarisk and olive. The patches of olive groves have a nice irony, for 'experts' scorn the biblical claim that the dove returned to the ark at Mount Ararat with an olive branch in its beak, claiming that no olives exist in that region. Well they do, near Artvin.

When the *dolmus* dropped me near the bridge at the bottom of the valley, I saw glimpses of buildings high up on the other side. Artvin is not picturesque: it is so steep that children have to play football on the dried-up river bed of the gorge below. Many of the buildings resemble barracks, which is what they are. As yet Artvin has no souvenir shops and the power falters constantly in the hotel. When the sun slides behind the mountains in the late afternoon the town is cast in shadow. Yet few places have entranced me more, for there is none of the alpine quaintness of Swiss towns. At night the lights are so high that you mistake them for stars; in the morning, the clouds swirl eerily around the town, only to disintegrate as the sun rises and proves the stronger.

A market of extraordinary vigour reflects Artvin's individuality. Strangers are viewed with bemused tolerance and the older men actually enjoy being photographed. The women are emancipated compared to Erzurum, unveiled and uninhibited, and the range of costumes worn by the peasants indicates the influences on this mountainous region, once so remote: Georgian, Persian, Kurd, Armenian, even Genoese. A dwarf is hoisted high by smiling friends as a symbol of good luck, a lemon clutched in each pudgy hand as he gesticulates for my camera, relishing his moment of attention.

The main event of the year is a marathon bullfight at the Kafkasor picnic site, the difference being that the bulls fight each other until the weaker has suffered enough and runs away. The event lasts for several days and delights the locals, though it dismays the stranger.

Like Erzurum, the town was occupied by the Russians for forty years until they handed it over to the Armenians when they withdrew towards the end of the First World War. Allegedly their cruelty was such that Turks fled from the town and hid in the forests until they took their revenge under Ataturk in 1921. It is hard to sort out the truth of these contrasting 'massacres' – probably it lies somewhere in between.

Discovering the ruins of early Georgian or Armenian churches is the real reward for exploring the countryside around Artvin. I sought the advice of my hotelier, Yavuz Karahan.

'I think the climb is not possible for you,' Yavuz advised me when I mentioned Porta, assessing my bulk with alarm. 'Porta is too steep, too difficult.' After this, I had to go there.

Enver, the gallant driver recommended by Yavuz, double-backed along a mountain track off the main road, assuring me in sign-language that this would bring us close to the final ascent. Judging by the falls of rock which we had to clear, and the height of the weeds, no vehicle had passed that way for months. The twists and turns were alarming, for pieces of the 'road' had fallen away. I hissed with fear as we scraped past with inches to spare and I saw breathtaking views of the gorge far below. Finally we were brought up short by a boulder too big for us to move. 'No problem,' cried Enver, and while I walked round on foot he skidded the car up the shale on the mountainside, almost turning it over in the process, and careered back down the other side of the boulder. He beamed as I joined him: 'No problem!'

But a few moments later he was defeated by an impassable rock-fall and we had to continue on foot. After a mile or so we reached a barn where a peasant woman was sharpening her husband's sickle, watched by two wide-eyed children. A grizzled old man wearing a turban allowed a passing boy to climb a tree and present us with a fruit which looked like a perfectly shaped, large green apple, yet proved as tough as teak.

By a fortunate coincidence it turned out that the boy lived in Porta. He was returning with a large bottle of sunflower oil and a cardboard box containing his shopping, for which he must have travelled a considerable distance. He showed us the way along a slippery path that frequently vanished altogether. The boy knew every foothold, but I was wretchedly out of condition and sweated profusely with beating heart in the thin mountain air on this scorching day in October. Several times I had to crawl on my hands and knees. If I had fallen down the slope I would have survived unless I struck a rock, but that was scant comfort.

As we climbed I wondered about those who chose to live such a self-sufficient existence in so remote a place – if you were old or had an accident, you would not be able to leave. The smiling, courteous boy was so silent I thought he might be a mute until I heard him whisper to Enver as they forged ahead of me.

And then the promise of Porta was fulfilled. First we made for a shaded well, from which I drank copiously of the pure spring water, more welcome than champagne. Then I took in that first startling glimpse of wooden chalets in pristine condition beside the church which the Governor of Ardanuc swears is of Genoese rather than Georgian or Armenian origin. A closer look reveals that the church is in danger of becoming a ruin unless some action is taken, but this is unlikely given its inaccessibility. Yet Porta once had a population of 10,000 people and was the first stop on the trade route south from Trebi-

zond. Yavuz believed there was a road two yards wide for some form of transport, though this is hard to imagine today: an uncanny silence reigned and there was no sign of life until I sensed a movement from scarcely a yard away and saw a herd of gentle, quizzical goats staring at me from their pen. The boy explained in mime that they belonged to himself and his family. Now I understood the softness of his voice; if someone shouted in Porta it would seem obscene.

Afterwards, Yavuz accounted for the curious absence of dogs in Porta. At this time of year the sheep are taken to a higher level to graze, and the dogs go with them to protect them from wolves. At night the peasants and dogs return to the lower village to guard it, particularly from marauding bears. A couple could ruin a garden of vegetables and fruit in a single evening, but the peasants cannot afford the licence required to shoot them.

Plainly the Genoese church, built of stone the colour of Devonshire cream, had been the pivot for the small community, offering a sense of reassurance that lingered even now.

Worth every drop of perspiration, every alarming heartbeat, Porta is an enchanted place.

After a lazy day recovering in Artvin I said goodbye at the hotel and drove with Enver up a reasonable if alarming road on the side of a barren mountain to the delightful village of Ishan at the top. The sudden views of its trees and flowers has the thrill of an oasis in the desert. Where Porta was timeless and still, almost moribund, Ishan was bustling with the activity of a community hard at work: a boy collected sweetcorn which fell from the sacks on the back of his donkey; an old woman washed her clothes in the stream, though she may not have been as old as she appeared; a man had climbed to the top of the ancient walnut tree beside the ruined church and was knocking the green fruit to the ground.

The exterior of the church at Ishan looks intact, so my first impression was one of pure elation and surprise. Ishan is a classic example of the Georgian style: perfect pro-

portions with elegant designs carved into the pale rose sandstone above the great wooden doors. Rebuilt on an earlier foundation (826), Ishan was the site of a bishopric until the seventeenth century. That anything remains of such churches is miraculous when you consider Turkish antagonism towards Christian relics in such a distant corner of their country. What is more, the Armenians were suspected of burying their gold in the foundations before they left, which often led to the use of dynamite. Today, the greatest hope for these churches, now on the verge of collapse, is the tourists who pay their respects, and more importantly, their money.

Yet Ishan, too, is off the tourist track, apart from the occasional tour, and the church was deserted as I wandered around, except for a boy who insisted on having his photograph taken. The sense of peace was overwhelming.

I left elated, saying goodbye to Enver at the crossroads where I could catch a bus to Kars. While I waited, two of the nastiest men I have seen staggered bleary-eyed from their car clutching guns, and demanded tea from the kiosk. The proprietor whispered to me that they were hunting bears. When I went to have a pee behind a nearby stack of wood one of them followed me and shouted '*Yok!*', shaking his head in apparent anger. I misjudged the man, for he gesticulated with his gun towards a row of beehives and explained in English: 'The bees will not be pleased.'

Looking at his gun, I doubted if the bears would be that thrilled, and raced off to catch the bus to Kars, which had just pulled up.

Kars enjoys the worst reputation of any town in Eastern Europe. Even Turks have assured me that it is dangerous to walk through the streets at night, and would not dare to do so themselves. Certainly Kars has endured extraordinary hardship, and bears the scars today, which makes its ebullience even more remarkable.

You step back in time to a provincial capital at the turn of the century, without the gentility depicted by Chekhov, but with the gusto of a frontier town. The atmosphere is Russian, which is hardly surprising, for the border is only a few miles away and Kars has always provided the key to Tiflis and Tanscaucasia. Seized by Tamburlaine in the fourteenth century, the town was occupied by the Russians in 1828, 1855 and in the war of 1877–8, an occupation which lasted until 1921.

The town is still dominated by the citadel, the ancient fortress where the English commander, General Fenwick Williams, fought with the Turks in the Crimean War. In Britain the nation was thrilled by accounts of the siege of Kars written by the Chief Medical Officer, Dr Humphry Sandwith, especially as the English losses were slight compared to those in the Crimea itself. However, the Turks realised that such a siege would end inevitably in defeat; they were outnumbered 15,000 to 30,000 by the Russians, the town was ravaged by a cholera epidemic and there was such hunger that soldiers dug up grass and ate the roots while horse-soup was reserved for the wounded. Starvation brought the siege to an end, but the surrender of the garrison was accompanied by chivalrous gestures from the English and the Russians. Dr Sandwith reported that the eyes of the two generals brimmed with tears 'whilst their hearts were big with the sentiments of high honour and graceful benevolence'. The gallantry was magnificent, although less so for the Turks who smashed their muskets against the battlements crying 'Long Live the Sultan!'

Kars still shows evidence of the Russian occupation and natural disasters such as earthquakes. Yet the few houses with any pretension to grace reveal a Russian influence, low and modest with the occasional cast-iron balcony and an art-nouveau design around a door. The new concrete buildings are discordant and ramshackle in contrast – give me the broken façade of former glory any time.

A taxi took me from the bus-stop to my hotel. All I remember is the horse-drawn traffic, the swarthy men in caps and long leather coats herding sheep into town along the muddy main street, a tug of war between a sheep that had been sold and its new owner, the geese parading with sublime indifference along the cracked pavement. Oh, the joy of finding nothing *modern* in Kars! – apart from those concrete blocks.

After a few hundred yards we turned into a gloomy back street where the driver got out. I waited, assuming that he was collecting a friend or delivering a message, with that admirable Turkish disdain for time. Instead, he signalled that this was my hotel, and the back street was, in fact, the smartest in Kars. The Temal Palas is so infamous that many have described it as one of the worst hotels in Eastern Europe and Turks shake their heads in shame when it is mentioned, but I felt it had been maligned. The place reeks of shabby gentility and boiled cabbage, but it is clean and my bedroom actually had a sit-down lavatory that worked.

I saw no other foreigner as I explored that evening accompanied by the serious boy who carried my luggage upstairs and refused to be detached after a too generous tip. Though hardly an inspiring companion, he proved useful with his smattering of English, which he was proud to practise as he led me around corners and showed me the shuttered, painfully neglected Armenian church which dates back to the eleventh century, now reduced to a lavatory and a dumping ground for rubbish.

I parted from the boy when I passed an immense beer-room with vast, naïve murals of shepherds, rearing horses and dramatic dogs, of such uninhibited sentimentality that they drew the eyes irresistibly. Unlike the cafés where occasional, tiny glasses of tea were brought from the back to the men playing board games, it served alcohol. A few doors along was the Samdan, a surprisingly imposing restaurant with a *fin de siècle* air. The customers included some of the toughest, shaven-headed, bearded Turks I had seen but the food was startlingly good.

There was only one drawback: it was 6.30 and the rest of the evening loomed with ominous boredom. What on earth should I do next? This was solved by eating a second dinner at a restaurant beyond the crossroads which mark the centre of the town. If this sounds like gluttony, I should stress that I only went there for dessert, to pass the time and write some notes.

The Granda was certainly grander than the Samdan. It was virtually empty apart from a gnarled old man who joined me at my table. He stared at me with a concentration that would seem rude in England, though not in Turkey, and we conversed politely, each unable to understand a word the other was saying. When I offered him a *raki* he smiled and pointed to his heart in refusal. This does not imply a heart condition, as I once assumed; it is the courteous yet decisive way of saying, 'No, thank you.' Rising to his feet he gave me a formal salute and returned to his table.

The lack of visible class distinctions is one of the pleasant surprises when travelling through Turkey. Because life is hard, with the shared need for survival, the boot-black and cobbler, the waiter, the farmer, and the hotel manager congregate on equal terms with the recognition that each is doing his best. The sense of family and respect for the older generation are paramount, with old peasants included in celebrations given by their wealthier sons and soignée daughters-in-law at smart restaurants, a contrast which would be unthinkable in snobbish England.

When a well-dressed group arrived at the Granda and one of the men introduced himself, I asked if there was any night-life – a fatuous question in a town where there is virtually a curfew, which made him laugh. He assumed I was looking for a night-club, but in fact I was thinking of something simpler and found it in one of the cafés next to the crossroads, where a group of men waved me over to their table and poured me a tumblerful of *raki*, which took immediate and devastating effect.

The Turks became exceedingly drunk, and I lost all sense of caution, allowing myself to be whirled off with them in a semi-stupor in a battered car which raced alarmingly through ruined streets on the outskirts of town. I gathered they were searching for a particular brothel in the district known as *genelever*, which means 'common houses'. No house looked intact, and when two of the Turks tumbled out, angered at having lost their way, they started to tussle in the rubble. I suggested in a sudden burst of sobriety that it might be a good idea to go back to our *raki*. I did not wish to be stranded in this surrealist wilderness with no sense of direction and no sign of life around me, yet our return deprived me of a visit to a Turkish brothel with the gargantuan, chiffoned ladies who appeal to Turkish men. I was ashamed the next morning when I remembered the warning in a guide-book that such a visit is 'an experience best reserved for the adventurous and not for the faint-hearted'. That I should be a faint-hearted traveller!

In her *Guide to Eastern Turkey* Diane Darke describes Kars as 'the armpit of Eastern Turkey', I found it tough, primitive but inordinately gallant. The men of Kars (I scarcely saw a woman) were remarkably hospitable considering that most foreigners only come here on their way to the ghost-city of Ani, a place that represents everything they hate, for Ani replaced Kars as the capital of Armenia in 961 until it was sacked by Tamburlaine.

Ani lies roughly 40 kilometres to the east, in the no-man's-land before the Russian frontier. The journey is uninspiring: a straight road crosses fields of dry thistles, hovering crows, and parallel telephone lines, a landscape that Hitchcock might have loved. A village with a pond and obligatory gaggle of geese set me wondering. Surely the geese are not kept as pets, like Turkish ducks. Filled with a sudden yearning for roast goose, I composed this ditty in the car:

> Geese and gander on parade
> In every village venue,

So why is it, do you suppose,
They're never on the menu?

At an army garrison I showed my permit and handed over my passport and camera, which were confiscated politely by the soldier in charge. After another stop at a *Jendarma* post we reached the gates of Ani and the remnants of a great walled city. These gates emblazoned with lions and swastikas are the first indication of Ani's importance. Once the equal of Cairo and Baghdad, it had a hundred gates, a thousand-and-one churches, and a population of 100,000, possibly twice that number at its peak. Ruled by Armenian war-lords, the city prospered as a staging post on the caravan route between the West and Persia. In 1319 a devastating earthquake shattered the city (as Leninakan just across the Russian frontier was destroyed in the winter of 1988); the Mongol raids of Tamburlaine then brought the final ruination. With a final inscription dated 1348, the city was abandoned. It was rediscovered in 1837 by an Englishman who reported that 'the shapeless mounds of Babylon are like the skeleton, yet the deserted city of Ani resembles the corpse whose breath has fled, but which still retains the semblance of life.' Perhaps he saw it on a sunny day when the grass was stirring in the wind. Perhaps a few people still lived there. Today there are just a couple of men at the gates who sell you photographs. Yet Ani does have a dormant quality, unlike the lifeless mounds of buried Troy.

'There is not much to see,' a tourist had warned me before I set out. She must have meant this literally, for there are barely a dozen buildings left of the thousands which existed before: yet, as you turn around, there is everything to see – an infinity of plain in one direction, the snow-capped mountains of Armenia, Mount Ararat to the south, and the land unfolding in front of you, broken by rifts and ravines. Russian watch-towers, a kilometre apart, rise facelessly with their guards obscured; the Arpa Cayi river swirls impassively through a deep gorge, forming part of the border; a Soviet garrison is only 500 yards away.

You are forbidden to climb the ancient citadel, but you can attempt a visit to St Gregory's Church (Resimli Kilise) built in 1215, perched on the edge of the ravine, with colourful murals inside and out, and carvings of peacocks, stags and dragons surrounded by foliage.

The grandiose cathedral, dating from the tenth century, stands in dramatic isolation. Built by the architect who repaired the dome of the Hagia Sophia in Constantinople when it was damaged in the earthquake of 989, it is the largest Armenian church in Turkey today, stark and forbidding with its black and ochre blocks of stone. Here is the melancholy of solitude.

I travelled from Kars to Doğubayazit by *dolmus*, which meant that we stopped erratically at the driver's whim. First a farmer raised a wistful, solitary hand, and took twenty minutes stuffing ten sacks of corn, four bails of hay, and a dozen wooden boxes into the boot. When we lumbered off again the door refused to close, so the farmer had to cling on to it until we reached the village of Kağizman, where he pushed everything out again while we had a glass of tea.

The passenger next to me was a little boy who became fearfully sick. All this is part of the fun of travelling by *dolmus* but it requires faith and this was tested when the shaky vehicle collapsed at Iğdir.

As I sat down for further tea, I gathered that a relief *dolmus* would take us on to Doğu-bayazit. A few minutes later a boy ran out of the depot's office and thrust a 1,000 lira note into my hand, with a serious shake of the head. A furious argument convulsed a group of passengers who were waiting too, and I gathered that the relief had broken down as well. They planned to continue by taxi and reluctantly accepted me as a fellow-passenger.

The taxi eventually arrived and as six of us scrambled inside, someone closed the door on the fingers of my right hand. They were not broken, but the pain was agonising. Four months later my nails were still black, though starting to fall off as new ones grew underneath.

It was dark when we took off. The men shouted at each other in the back until there was a sudden silence and one of them hit me on the shoulder.

'Alman?'

'No, I am English,' I informed him primly.

'Ah. I speak leetle English. So you go to Iran?'

'I most certainly do not.' I shuddered at the idea.

'Yes, you do. We all go to Iran, we are Iranians.'

Slightly hysterical by now, I accepted that pain and disaster are part of travel. 'No problem!' I cried, happy that I was no longer just a tourist but a sort of traveller at last, the adventure compensating for the lost bordello in Kars.

Sadly it ended in Doğubayazit, where the Iranians stopped to buy sugar, margarine and oil, which are cheaper than across the border. The town teems with Iranian families – angry bearded men and veiled women, shouting at each other in apparent argument, staying in small hotels with names like Tahran. Now that the war is over, Doğubayazit is once again on the trade route between East and West. For me it lacked the charm of Kars. Trailing children cried 'Meestair, baksheesh,' shopkeepers asked for dollars; the older men cringed from my camera and waved me away angrily. The gloomy *lokantas* do not serve alcohol but the Hotel Isfahan was comfortable. There rich young Iranians in jeans, on their way by car to shop for jewellery in Istanbul, drank whisky and openly condemned the Ayatollah as a 'madman', while a peasant family in traditional robes demanded a prayer mat which they placed in the direction of Mecca, just outside the lavatory. A large mirror faced them on the wall opposite, so they appeared to be praying to themselves.

There was also the anomaly of high-pitched English voices as I came down to breakfast:

'Good morning! And how did you sleep?'

'Terribly. My bed was so hard I had a bad dream every time I moved.'

'How *dreadful*! Do have an olive, they're delicious.'

'I'd rather have marmalade.'

'We've just walked into town and found the most marvellous market.'

'Oh, you're both so adventurous.'

I cringed in my corner, concealed behind a book, or so I thought until I heard my name, followed by whispers.

'I'm sure it is.'

'Who did you say?'

Finally, a charming man came over, apologised for disturbing me, and said, 'I just wanted to thank you for writing *A Traveller in Turkey*! After reading it, the wife and I were determined to come to Turkey for ourselves, and here we are!'

Totally disarmed, I felt ashamed of my stand-offishness. That a book of mine should have such a positive result is a rare reward.

I waved goodbye as their group boarded the Sunquest coach for Lake Van, not really minding that I was a fellow-tourist once again.

If the camera cannot lie, the photographer certainly can. I have seen pictures of Isak Pasha's palace floating over the lonely plain, an image of such beauty that it haunted my imagination. But the approach is prosaic, through the suburbs of Doğubayazit; miraculously, the camera deletes the electricity pylons and the ugly, square concrete boxes which mar the foreground, and photographers are shrewd enough to time their snaps when there is neither car nor human being in sight, much less coaches, taxis or caravans.

Despite all this, Isak Pasha *is* romantic. Here is Xanadu, a stately pleasure dome with a stream which may indeed be sacred. Of all the mosques and palaces in the Middle East, Isak Pasha is closest to my image of the Arabian Nights. It looks as old as time, with Mount Ararat as a backdrop. In fact it is comparatively modern, started by Isak Pasha in 1784 and completed by his son. Serving as a customs house on the silk road from Persia, it made Isak Pasha so wealthy that he was able to decorate the inside of his palace sumptuously. The disparate styles – Seljuk, late Ottoman, baroque – come together as an inspired entity. The harem, described today as 'the women's quarters', offers little evidence of former sensual delight, but the Feast Room with its columns and black and white walls suggests the famous banquets they consumed. An ambassador from Persia was entertained so lavishly that when he reached Constantinople he told the sultan, Selim II, that Isak Pasha's palace put all the rest to shame – a tactless comparison.

The morning I visited the palace the great plain was darkening from an approaching storm, and the pale pink walls of the palace glowed in radiant contrast, one of the loveliest sights I have seen. Climbing the hill behind Isak Pasha, it looked as dramatic as the images which had haunted me, and I, too, was careful to crop the ugly telephone poles in the foreground.

As I returned to Doğubayazit, I glimpsed the summit of Mount Ararat before it was obscured by the swirling clouds, and then the heavens broke and all grew hazy in the rain. But when I left two mornings later, the lower slopes were shining in the sun and the summit, capped with white, beckoned. I could understand the compulsion to climb mountains with the need to find, or lose, yourself in another dimension.

Mount Ararat, the most evocative of names, where the deluge stopped and we survived, has a majesty which surpasses lesser peaks and exudes a sense of serenity which is infinitely satisfying. I was glad to have seen the whole of Ararat shining clear, for that is a rarity, and looked back several times for a final reassurance. And then we turned away and the mountain was lost.

A Corpse in the Adriatic –
and Two Mystery Ladies
in Urbino

'Have you heard of the body floating in the sea?' Angela Carter asked me on my final day at the Mysfest in Cattolica.

Mysfest? Cattolica? The first I knew of either was a phone call from a woman who sounded so exaggeratedly sexy that I suspected a hoax.

'I wish talk Meestair Fearson,' she began.

'You are,' I replied, suspiciously.

'I am Barbara and invite you to meet some Mystery Ladies.'

'Oh, yes,' I replied sarcastically, thinking for a fleeting moment of the whores in Genoa.

'And your presence will be very precious.'

'Not too precious, I hope,' a quip which deservedly fell on stony Italian soil. She explained that she was phoning from Roma to invite me to the annual horror film festival on the Adriatic. Mystery Ladies were the main theme for the 1988 Mysfest, and Jack the Ripper another. As I am supposed to be an expert on this latter subject, my suspicions were disarmed and I accepted on impulse. It sounded daft enough to be fun, though I had my doubts when the man who runs the Lina Stores in Soho described Cattolica as 'Southend on Adriatic – only worse'.

Cattolica is a ninety-minute drive from Bologna airport along a grim, built-up motorway. The town might have been charming once, though I doubt if it was ever beautiful. Fishing boats still tie up at one end hinting at past activity, but today the lengthy beach is scored with parallel lines of mats and umbrellas, patrolled by swarthy beachmen who greet the sunbathers with exaggerated cries of *'Buon giorno!'* and the charm of basking

Angela Carter, Mark Pearce and their son on the beach at Cattolica.

sharks. The sands are overshadowed by a battery of hotels with names like the Splendid, the Bristol and the London, built in the post-war boom when the coastline was a cheap new pleasure-ground and Englishwomen arrived in search of Latin lovers, and many stayed.

I was booked into the Victoria Palace, which proved less hilarious than its name, with a room cringing from a dreadful, peeling wall a few yards opposite my tiny balcony, which revealed a glimpse of shallow sea if I leant over it, and figures 'swimming' in discoloured water up to their ankles. Arriving at two in the morning, I was hurried to the Casanova Club where Barbara from Roma fulfilled her sexy voice, and I performed a weary, elephantine disco dance with Susannah York, one of the 'stars' of the Mysfest, who regarded me with the crisp disapproval of a neat nanny. Peering bleary-eyed from my balcony the next morning, the day was sunless and the rain poured down.

Mystery Ladies turned out to be a euphemism for women crime-writers. Angela Carter seemed mysterious and a cut above the rest of us as a serious novelist and a member of the International Film Jury. When I suggested a gory background for a photograph, she declined frostily while smiling warmly: 'I could not do that as a guest of the Municipality.' I thought her stuck-up until I visited the hotel where she was staying with her friend Mark Pearce, and was more relaxed. Their son, Alexander, looking more Italian than any *bambino* on the beach, smiled at the camera with the easy charm of a film-star.

Reluctant to discuss the Mysfest, in her role as honoured guest, she admitted that her friends did not associate her with this sort of place, 'But I love it! I see two films a day and they look much better in a foreign language. Only the Italians could get away with this. To say they take it seriously sounds too Germanic, but they enjoy it with a touch of irony too. It's a wonderful way of filling up the town.' I remarked that this was one of several such festivals along the Adriatic; the next one was devoted to romance, using a pink rose as the logo. She shuddered. 'I think the Mysfest is more my sort of thing.' Our logo was a headless man in a white raincoat and hat reminiscent of Humphrey Bogart.

The Mysfest was disappointingly sedate – no rash of horror starlets with artificial fangs, pouting to the pop of champagne corks and the flash of paparazzi. The films were shown in the late afternoon and evening and included Claude Chabrol's sensual *Le Cri du Hibou* (*The Cry of the Owl*), with his usual lingering emphasis on meals. When I was introduced and had explained why I was there, he embraced me cheerfully – 'Jack ze Ree-pair! Oh zat wonnerful man!'

The cheerfulness began to grow on me, especially at night when the streets were crowded with promenading film fans and the shops displayed the Mysfest colours of black and yellow. I drank relays of Campari and fresh orange juice at the outside cafés and watched the watchers; I soon found I was starting to enjoy the vulgarity of Cattolica, which was unabashed. The food in the crowded, noisy cafés was superb, especially heaped platefuls of spaghetti with clams and generous Parmesan.

But why had the three Ripperologists not been invited to the best seafood restaurant on the harbour along with the Mystery Ladies? Why did Irene Bignardi, the director of the Mysfest dress like a vampire? Why did the lady novelists find yellow roses in their bedrooms except for one whom everyone hated, an unfortunate novelist called Janet? Why did Janet then disappear? And what of the body discovered floating in the sea? This was part of the festival gossip.

In the small enclosure where a TV camera waited inertly for live interviews by day, and stars gathered volubly for drinks at night in a parody of Cannes, I met two of the most formidable Mystery Ladies – Margaret Yorke (*Speak for the Dead*) and Dorothy Uhnak (*Victim*). We agreed to visit Urbino the following day.

Splendid in their contrast, Margaret Yorke was sensibly dressed with neat grey hair, scurrying through the streets of Cattolica as if she were late for tea with an old school chum at Ye Copper Kettle, as shrewd and sharp-eyed as Miss Marple. Dorothy, a smiling, motherly woman, followed in her wake, but there was nothing quaint about them, as our conversation in the taxi revealed.

I had not read Margaret Yorke before; now I agree with those who regard her as the equal of P. D. James, and the more surprising. Abrasively intelligent and a Shakespearian scholar, she slipped quotations into her speech at the Mysfest, though she doubted if anyone recognised them. Her books reflect the harsh new realism started by Patricia Highsmith. 'My latest,' she informed me, 'has a lesbian, though I didn't realise she was going to become one. I've yet to tackle incest, but I shall.' Yorke offers no conventional clues, no butlers, no final revelation to assembled guests on chintz-covered sofas. Instead she plays a teasing game – the young man who seems so decent is just out of prison; the grieving widow has murdered her husband; the man who is plainly innocent is not. Few of her characters are what they seem and deserve no sympathy except that they are vulnerable like the rest of us. Like Chabrol she strips the veneer from provincial life though her characters tend to survive on frozen lasagne and beans in contrast to his obsession with haute cuisine. It's a bleak outlook from someone so jolly.

With thirty books to her credit, her success is the more gratifying for being belated. She had just returned from a crime writers' conference in New York when she received the invitation to go to Cattolica.

'My first words were "how long?" When they said a full week I could hardly believe it. I'm having a wonderful holiday with all expenses paid and all I have to do is make a speech for twenty minutes and try to be civil.'

Dorothy Uhnak was a New York cop for fourteen years. She was wearing a replica of her shield: 'I ended in the fourteenth precinct as Detective Second Grade. . .'

'Don't sell yourself short, Dorothy,' interrupted Margaret sharply. 'Second is *very* good.'

Margaret had established her supremacy in the taxi as self-appointed guide: 'I told Dorothy she simply had to see Urbino or she'd fail to see the true Italy. Look, Dorothy, look, that's *exactly* the sort of view you see in the background of Italian paintings.'

Dorothy looked obediently, though I noticed that she gritted her teeth. I discovered the reason when we walked up the slope to the Ducal Palace, and she limped. 'Are you in pain?' I asked.

'Considerable. Usually I wear a steel brace but that's difficult in a small car.' Her injury dated from the time a prisoner tried to escape and threw her down an escalator. She then went back to work earlier than she should have done, to prove her equality with her male colleagues in the force. In New York a few months before the Mysfest, a man on a motor-bike tried to snatch her bag and she was thrown on to her injured knee. Now she faced two operations, after a forthcoming conference in Russia.

Her portrait in the Mysfest brochure showed a vulnerable-looking black-haired girl. Her appearance was part of her strength as a policewoman when she made her arrests: 'They underestimated me because I didn't act as I looked. They didn't know I was a tough girl; now I'm the little old lady who takes in all the strays.'

When I mentioned this blend of toughness and sentimentality to Angela Carter she was not surprised: 'I thought all New York cops were like that.' I noticed, however, that while Dorothy's calling card was headed *The Mighty Minkey Production Company* after a favourite cat, Angela's was illustrated with Betty Boop.

Today, Dorothy Uhnak is rich beyond the dreams of British authors, with the paperback rights of *The Investigation* selling for 1,600,000 dollars. With touches of the same black humour and ultimate morality of Chandler, her books give no indication that the author is a woman. 'I keep my picture off the covers since a reader protested, "How can such a pretty face write about such horrible things?"'

'A journalist asked the same of me,' said Margaret. 'I told him I haven't *always* been a grandmother.'

Listening to them in a quiet back garden of a restaurant opposite the Ducal Palace, I wondered how they would react if somebody stood in their way. A brusque verdict on poor Janet, whose travellers' cheques were stolen from her hotel bedroom before her disappearance, revealed Margaret's impatience: 'Born victim!' she declared.

'Have you ever killed anyone, Dorothy – when you were a cop, I mean?' It seemed a strange question in such surroundings, but I had seen her temper when my fellow-Ripperologist, Martin Fido, appeared in a T-shirt depicting the Ripper's victims.

'What next?' she snarled. 'Mutilation of small children, that would be *real* cute.' Turning to me, she asked if I might feel differently if the Ripper had been a woman and draped the male genitals over the victim's corpse.

'Yes, Dorothy, I would,' I agreed hastily.

Now she admitted that on three occasions she came close to killing. 'Once when a culprit put a gun to my head and I knocked him down and took him into custody. When the prisoner threw me down the moving escalator: I held my gun against his head but then I realised he was totally insane, and he escaped. The third time, instead of shooting I slammed the man with my gun butt and he cried, "You little SOB, what did you hit me with?" "My gun," I told him, but he'd fainted by then. I was cautioned afterwards – "You should have shot the bastard." Kill someone? Yes, I think so, if there was no alternative.'

Margaret agreed: 'I could kill in defence of a threatened grandchild, or possibly in self-defence.'

On my return I checked back with Angela Carter, who looked as if she was expecting my visit. 'No further details, I'm afraid. Frankly, I don't think a corpse in the sea off a summer resort is terribly sinister, perhaps somebody going for a swim too soon after lunch, poor thing. All the same it gives a *frisson*. The latest rumour says the body floated down from Rimini.' Though still unidentified, that seemed to dispose of Janet. Angela Carter was smiling mysteriously when I left, and something made me turn back:

'Would *you* be capable of killing someone?'

'Oh, Dan!' She laughed dismissively. 'They have to hold me back.'

In Cattolica there was a curious magic in the air which led to an instant rapport between myself, Margaret Yorke, Dorothy Uhnak and Magda Napp, who lives in Florence and regaled me with tales of the Transvestite Murderer and the Monster of Florence who preys on courting couples. That rapport can be the joy of holidays, too, when you have the chance to meet people who would not usually swim in your stretch of the water. 'We must keep in touch,' they always say. It is rare to do so, but I have kept up with my three Mystery Ladies – and Angela Carter, my leading suspect.

The Art of Death

One of the kindest editors I have worked for was the late John Anstey. Many contributors could not stand him because he ran the *Sunday Telegraph Magazine* like a one-man band. Legendary for correcting the punctuation of Graham Greene, he demanded interminable revisions, which I was happy to accept providing I saw the cheque at the end of the rewrite. Also, I had a genuine respect for Anstey and welcomed his comments. Sharing his aversion to the telephone, I was grateful for the punctilious way in which he answered every letter by return, if only to say that he would be writing in greater detail the following day.

At one point I came up with an idea which most editors would have turned down flat – a survey of graveyard art in Europe. The extravagance of such a project appealed to him and he asked me to call at his palatial office, an honour considering his dislike of confrontation. He was a powerful man, or gave this impression, and his slight shyness lent him considerable charm. Offering me a drink, he accepted my idea instinctively. It embraced a wide area, starting in Highgate Cemetery, then so overgrown that reports of foxes and black magic among the Victorian statuary were wholly credible; and finishing at the English cemetery of Sulina on the edge of the Black Sea, commemorating the British Commission that existed here after the First World War, and men who 'Drowned in the Danube' or 'Died from the effects of climate'.

There was one aspect I dared not raise, though the story depended on it – the problem of 'expenses'. Anstey was civilised enough to sense this, and, speaking as if I were doing him the favour, he asked if it would help to have some money. The funds he provided were a vital lifeline.

I set out across Europe in an open Triumph, probably the only car I have actually liked, accompanied by a young man and his girl-friend who acted as driver. They became increasingly dismayed as I dragged them into every cemetery I could find, running after funerals, joining a procession of wailing peasants in Yugoslavia, lying spread-eagled over a Venetian bridge to photograph a gondola hearse laden with flowers. They may have hoped for a jolly holiday, but I became increasingly obsessed with death.

The reason for the journey was valid: I was genuinely fascinated by graveyard art and the conflicting attitudes to death. I have never understood the need for graveyards to be lugubrious or funeral services to be so sombre, when death above all is inevitable. If the dead man or woman has led a rich and worthwhile life, surely this is a cause for celebration? At least the Victorians adorned their cemeteries with monuments and gardens, even if the overgrowth added a Gothic melancholy. Why not a happy cemetery? I set out to find one.

My interest in the art of the graveyard was inspired by my first glimpse of Genoa and the amazing hillside of the Staglieno which I visited briefly when the ship stopped there on my first journey to Istanbul. The cemetery echoes the days when the port was the centre for wealthy merchants who employed the leading sculptors of the day to immortalise them or their families. Layered in terraces, surrounded by hedges of myrtle and cypress trees, the cemetery was designed by Carlo Baralino, who died in 1835 before the work had started. Visiting the main building, which housed 60,000 corpses, in 1877, Mark Twain was astounded:

> We shall continue to remember it after we have forgotten the palaces . . . on every slab is an inscription – for every slab covers a corpse . . . monuments, tombs and sculpted figures that are exquisitely wrought and full of grace and beauty. They are new and snowy; every outline is perfect, every feature guiltless of mutilation, flaw or blemish; and therefore to us these far-reaching ranks of bewitching forms are a hundredfold more lovely than the damaged and dingy statuary they have saved from the wreck of ancient art, and set up in the galleries of Paris for the worship of the world.

Twain went there when the Staglieno was comparatively new. On my short visit the 'sculpted figures' still looked 'snowy', due to a light covering of fine dust. The sculpture is wholly serious and the effect is moving in its genuine simplicity: a wife holds up the sheet for a last look at her husband; the family are collected around a deathbed; a widower clasps his eyes in grief as he stands against the tall, domed monument; a mother lifts up her child towards her husband for a final kiss. If this is sentimental, flattery is avoided and old ladies are remembered with a brutal realism.

My favourite tomb has a seated woman with a definite resemblance to Queen Victoria, waiting for her husband to join her in the adjacent space. A wealthy merchant, he honoured her proudly, but when his own turn came the money had gone and she waits alone. From a distance she looks mournful, almost severe, but when I drew closer I saw

a quizzical expression, almost a twinkle, which implies, 'I've seen it all. I don't mind waiting a little longer, boring though it can be.'

Our journey began in Paris, where most of the green patches on a map are not parks but cemeteries marked with crosses, providing dark pools of tranquillity in the midst of the din. If you wish for solitude in Paris you can find it among the dead. Père-Lachaise, named after a confessor to Louis XIV, covers a hundred acres, extended in 1804 from a garden which belonged to the Jesuits. This is the celebrities' graveyard, the final resting place for Colette, Chopin, Sarah Bernhardt, Edith Piaf, and of course for Oscar Wilde. Epstein's tomb was smaller and darker than I expected, though still impressive. A closer look revealed that the figure's testicles had been emasculated, surely an unfortunate embellishment in the first place, and beneath the broken stump someone had scratched the message: 'Miss you Mike, love Antonio 71.' Poor Oscar! He might have been amused, but I rather doubt it.

Montparnasse was hemmed in by the backs of buildings but contained one delightful tomb in the shape of a large double-bed with the husband and his wife in their night-clothes. The expression on the man's face as he sits up is of such weariness that it defies ridicule.

Montmartre was deeply depressing, dark with rows of mausoleums and cats crouching forbiddingly on the black stone. No one else in sight, everything dank and desolate. My next cemetery provided the antidote I had been searching for. It was on an island in the middle of the Seine, with trees and shrubs sloping down to the water on either side. The graves were small and the dates short lived, for this is a cemetery for dogs. I made a rough translation of one of the inscriptions:

> Willy our only friend. MOPSIK 1926-38
> Dear little Mopsik, so brave and affectionate, so faithful and so much better than us who have repaid all the generosity of your tender, noble heart by having you killed! Because old and ill you suffered, and we suffered with you. Dear Mopsik, forgive your ungrateful masters – their pain is infinite.

Sentimental? Of course. Pathetic? Perhaps, yet no less forlorn than those heartbreaking words on the graves of Flanders: 'He shall not have died in vain.'

My camera was protected from the drizzle in a carrier bag when I paid my entrance fee at the kiosk. As I was about to photograph the grave of a French Blacky – having an English Blacky back home – the concierge descended, accusing me of deliberate subterfuge in a storm of '*interdits*' and hysterical screams. When I declined to give her my camera, she resorted to a brow-clasping performance worthy of Madame Bernhardt, and ordered two uneasy gardeners to escort me out. She appealed to a passer-by, explaining that I was mocking the graveyard. The man looked at me aghast and assured her that he was an animal lover himself. 'Thank God!' she cried. I put a finger to my lips, urging her in a whisper to remember where she was, which was hardly helpful.

Outside the gates, shivering with anger, I hailed a taxi. The driver was a woman with that splendid Parisian mixture of chic and efficiency. I explained what had happened and by a strange coincidence one of her last passengers had brought his dog from Lyons to be buried in another animal cemetery near the airport, which she offered to show me. When we arrived she had a quick word with the concierge, whipped out a black head-scarf, and posed instinctively beside the graves. 'They cost as much as they do for a human being,' she told me. 'Go ahead and photograph, you will find no problem here.'

On the long drive back to St Germain she encouraged me to stop at the large Inter-communal Cemetery – for human beings – which was laid out as a garden. To my horror, she rushed up to one of the graves, seized some dead flowers and threw them aside. Then she picked up one of the framed photographs at the foot of the tomb and thrust it into my hand. 'My daughter,' she explained. I looked at a lovely, smiling, hopeful girl, who had been killed a few months earlier. There were tears in my eyes as I expressed my sympathy, which released a deluge of her own as she kissed the other photographs. 'My husband,' she said, '*and* my son.' The richly decorated marble grave must have cost a fortune in taxi fares and tips.

Then this remarkable woman wiped her tears and drove me back to St Germain. I intended to reward her with a handsome tip but she was adamant that she would accept nothing at all, until I saw a florist opposite, handed her my camera to look after, and returned with a lavish bunch of flowers, either for herself or her deceased.

Leaving Lyons, we turned west and drove to Hautrives through a tranquil countryside of green fields splashed with yellow mustard. When we reached the silent village with dogs stretched out in the shade, impervious to my approach, I followed the signs to the Palais Idéal, which I assumed, without much enthusiasm, was some sort of governmental building. Then I turned a corner and gasped.

The name was the literal truth. The local postman, Ferdinand Cheval, had created a palace out of his imagination. After it was finished he wrote a brief paper declaring his aim:

> A peasant, son of peasants, I wish to live and die to prove that even in my category there are men of genius and force. For twenty-nine years I have been the local postman. This work which is my glory and honour is my only happiness . . . a dream which has become a reality forty years later.

The scale of the palace is startling – twenty six metres long and built in several tiers, surrounded by trees and a peaceful garden. The grottoes are decorated with Cheval's 'bizarre' sculptures – three giants, the Virgin Mary and an Unknown Hero in a pantheon, a crocodile, pelicans and a young fawn. The effect is wonderful, beautiful and surreal, because the entire palace looks as if it is melting. One façade that Cheval referred to as a cascade conveyed a sense of writhing movement which is instantly reminiscent of Gaudí's cathedral in Barcelona, though it is unlikely that either man would have heard of the other, proof that similar ideas can be 'in the air' at the same moment.

Le Facteur Cheval was born in 1836 and died in 1924. He had no experience:

> I was treated as a fool; I was not a mason, I had never touched a trowel; as for sculpture, I did not know how to use a chisel; as for architecture, I had not spoken to anyone about it, nor studied it. I said nothing to anyone for fear of being ridiculed, and I experienced enough ridicule myself.

In his notes he describes how he came to realise his dream. He tripped over a stone 'formed in such a bizarre way that I put it in my pocket to admire at leisure'. To the annoyance of his wife, he started collecting them:

> The next day I passed the same spot and again picked up the most beautiful stone in the place. This was a stone like molasses worked by the elements and hardened by time, like flint. It was a sculpture so bizarre it is impossible for man to imitate. It represents all species of animals, all types of caricature.

With wheelbarrows of cement and larger stones from a nearby ravine, he started work. The labour is recorded in the bombastic inscriptions which marked his progress:

>1879-1913
>10 thousand working days
>93 thousand hours
>33 years of proof
>and the stubbornness which has gone into my work.

Other proclamations include:

>The source of wisdom is only through finding true happiness
>With a valiant heart nothing is impossible
>Where one dreams it becomes reality

Cheval has been called a 'primitive' and this is true in that he was self-taught, but he had a sophisticated genius ahead of his time and even of his own knowledge.

The postman completed his palace when he was sixty-nine. He then spent the next ten years constructing his tomb in the local cemetery. I somehow doubt that Cheval had a sense of humour, but his tomb is irresistibly comic, dominating the conventional graves as a fitting memorial to a man obsessed. If Cheval was one of the great accidental humorists in the history of art, this was his last laugh. On the door are the simple but lofty words he chose for himself: THE TOMB OF SILENCE AND ETERNAL REST. The villagers mocked him when Cheval was alive, but they charge admission to his palace now.

I continued to Venice and the island cemetery of San Michele, finding the graves of Diaghilev and Stravinsky close to each other in an overgrown corner. Stravinsky's has a rare simplicity, just his surname and IGOR underneath, though he was honoured with one of the last great public funerals by gondola. I hurried to the undertakers to ask if there was any chance of seeing a funeral by gondola along the canals, but learnt that these are now reserved for state occasions, unless a wealthy family makes a private arrangement. Disappointed, I was on my way to catch a vaporetta when I noticed a black and gold gondola moored beside some steps, laden with flowers. Sure enough, a few moments later, the funeral procession poured from the church opposite and continued by gondola, although it was motorised.

From then on I encountered funerals as if by arrangement with the above. On a dirt track in Yugoslavia, having lost my way, I noticed something stirring in the lazy village. Horse-drawn carts were arriving with women dressed in black. I assumed that all old peasant woman dressed in black, until I saw the church around the corner. As if it had been waiting for me, the procession began to move, led by a young man carrying a wooden cross. A terrible wailing broke out all around me, fierce, unrestrained cries that rent the air. I clicked away, appalled to realise the smile of elation on my face as the scene came into focus.

By the time I arrived in Athens I thought my preoccupation with death had been satiated. I was sitting in a square in Piraeus when it beckoned again. Outside the church opposite, wreaths were tied to banners with flowing purple sashes and men stood gossiping like seedy waiters smoking fags in a brief off-duty moment. Suddenly they stamped out their cigarettes, assumed expressions of utmost gravity and went inside. A few moments later they emerged wearing white gloves and carrying the coffin to the black funeral car decorated with gold fittings and eagles. My now blasé attitude was shattered by a swift, terrifying glimpse of the corpse through a small window in the coffin – an old grey-haired woman, her face twisted in agony, open-mouthed, without teeth.

I eventually found what I had been searching for in a muddy Romanian village on the borders of Russia. Sapinta is the home of a primitive artist called Stan Patras, who works in wood. The outside of his house was decorated with pictures, including one of the first space-ship, manned by Uri Gagarin, while the inside was dominated by a gigantic head of himself carved out of rock by his pupils. The walls were hung with portraits on wood of the Romanian cabinet, a popular singer and Christ.

Patras looked like a stocky, prosperous farmer; plainly he was a true naïve, and when I asked him, through a student who acted as interpreter, why he had started such work, he smiled: 'Like a child wanting to do something new. No school, no nothing, only my own talent.'

My two companions bought me one of his small wooden portraits – a man in peasant costume holding a bottle – as a present; it is one of the few possessions I have not sold or lost.

Around the corner was the work of art that makes Patras unique – a conventional graveyard around a church, filled with crosses of his own design. The first was made for a friend in 1935, now there are two hundred, each one decorated with a picture and a verse by Patras underneath.

Far from being reverent towards the deceased, the verses are unexpectedly honest. If the man was a drunk, he was shown with a glass in his hand. A mercenary woodcutter was shown with a tree falling on top of him and a verse below which concluded: 'Till I was young I was a good man and a good shepherd, but when I grew up I went another way. In a wood I chopped trees for better wages. I worked for only a few days before Death found me there. I was only twenty-two years old.'

Patras could be a devastating memorialist: 'I lived here fifty-five years, oh, how bored I am staying here. My name is Saulic Ion . . . I was tending sheep, I was becoming a bad man. I was shot in the head and afterwards I was decapitated. Like this they buried me, to be damned for ever.'

Instead of resenting such candour, the families asked Patras for a cross and left the verse to him; as he knew all the people in the village he was able to choose the characteristic by which the deceased would be remembered, for good or bad. Such frankness in an English graveyard would be exquisite.

Most of the verses are jollier than those I have quoted and the total effect, with the bright blue and reds beneath the trees and a triangular shape at the top carved with flowers, is wonderfully refreshing. A leading Romanian art critic, Petru Comarnescu, described Sapinta as *'cimitirul vesel'* – the happy cemetery. I had found it at last.

Dracula Country

I had another reason for being in Romania: Bram Stoker was a great-uncle and I was anxious to follow in his fictional footsteps and see the Transylvanian landscape which he described so brilliantly in the opening of *Dracula*.

I had already visited Whitby, where the vampire supposedly ran up the steps to the graveyard in the guise of a massive dog after his ship had been hurled ashore during a storm. Seated on one of the benches where Dracula enjoyed his first taste of Lucy, the scene matched the written description and the early photographs by Sutcliffe so closely that I might have been superimposing a negative on one of his prints. Only the garish noise from an amusement arcade on the quayside below marked the difference. I wanted to see if the same applied to Stoker's setting for Castle Dracula.

Also I was fascinated by Stoker himself. He wrote eighteen books but *Dracula* was his single triumph, though he was unaware of it then. He remains one of the least known authors of one of the best known books.

After a lifetime in the wings, managing the Lyceum Theatre for Sir Henry Irving, Stoker retired to Cruden Bay north of Aberdeen where he had written most of *Dracula*. Now so poor he could no longer afford to stay in the hotel, he rented a fisherman's cottage instead. Lame and half blind, his former strength had been sapped by his friendship with Irving, who was something of a vampire himself, and by the syphilis – general paralysis of the insane – which killed him.

When Count Dracula was cornered in Piccadilly, he rounded on his pursuers, snarling 'You think you have left me without a place to rest, but I have more. My revenge is just begun! I spread it over centuries, and *time is on my side*.' As Stoker limped across

Cruden Sands with his nice, strong walking stick, broken in health and fortune, I hope he realised that time was on his side too, yet I doubt if even his imagination could have conceived that he had created one of the myths of the twentieth century with *Dracula*, and spawned an industry around it.

Drac-ula! It is possible to imagine Stoker's relish when he first heard the name, from the Hungarian professor and explorer, Arminius Vambery, who may well have been the inspiration for the fictional Van Helsing. Irving and Stoker entertained Vambery in their private room in the Lyceum, The Beefsteak Club, on 30 April 1890. Stoker asked Vambery if he knew the meaning of fear:

'Fear of death – no; but I am afraid of torture. I protected myself against that, however.'

'How did you manage that?'

'I had always a poison pill, fastened here, where the lappet of my coat now is . . .'

During one of their meetings Vambery told Stoker of the superstitions in Transylvania, of vampires, and the bloodthirsty warrior, Dracula, Prince Vlad V of Wallachia who lived from 1431 to 1476. He was also known as Vlad the Impaler (Vlad Tepes in Romanian, *Tzepa* meaning spike), due to his habit of impaling his Turkish enemies on tall spikes – an excruciating torture. He was bloodthirsty even for his own time. An early print shows him devouring a meal beneath the impaled with apparent nonchalance. When a boyar dared to comment on the screams and smells, Vlad had him impaled on a taller stake – 'Up yonder, where the stench cannot reach you.' He forced mothers to eat their babies; when his mistress said she was pregnant he split her open to prove it; he invited the beggars of one city to a sumptuous meal, locked the doors and set fire to the place with the excuse of preventing plague and eliminating inferior stock; and when some visiting ambassadors neglected to doff their turbans, he had them nailed to their heads, a lesson in etiquette that was emulated by Ivan the Terrible.

Yet Vlad was a great warrior, killing 20,000 Turks after one battle in 1456. After another victory over the infidel, the bells of Christendom rang out in celebration as far off as the island of Rhodes.

Dracula means son of Dracul, and Dracul also means dragon, so Dracula can also be interpreted as son of the dragon. Vlad's father was a member of the Order Draconis, founded by the Holy Roman Emperor Sigismund, which sported a cross and a dragon on a crest. Bram Stoker seized on the name *Dracula* and acknowledged the warrior in his novel: 'One of my own race who as Viovode crossed the Danube and beat the Turk on his own ground! This was a Dracula indeed!' These were the words of Count Dracula who bears a resemblance to an early woodcut known as the Innsbruck portrait of Vlad: 'The mouth, so far as I could see under the heavy moustache, was fixed and rather cruel looking, with peculiarly sharp white teeth.' Many experts, including members of the Dracula Society, claim that Stoker based Count Dracula on Vlad the Impaler, and of course he took the name and certain aspects of Vlad's background, but Vlad was a national hero, whereas the Count was a vampire.

When I arrived in Bucharest (founded by Vlad in 1458 as a citadel) for the first time in

1972, I was welcomed as Stoker's great-nephew, though his name was comparatively new and *Dracula* had never been published there apart from a magazine serial in 1928.

'It is a delicate affair,' said the Minister for Propaganda, and the other men around the table in his office sighed and nodded their agreement. They were just beginning to realise the tourist potential of Dracula Tours but they feared that in promoting the Count, their national hero would be labelled as a vampire. Their fears have been justified to the point where the fictional Count has eclipsed the hero.

Mr George, a charming, bulky man with tragic eyes and smudges underneath, offered to act as our guide that afternoon. At Lake Snagov, a few miles to the north, we crossed by boat to the small island monastery where Vlad Dracula is allegedly buried, although his death is surrounded in controversy. When his tomb at Snagov was opened in 1931 it was empty, though there were rumours of a headless skeleton, which is correct historically: Vlad's head was severed and sent to the Sultan in Constantinople as proof that the Impaler was dead. Near Galata Bridge in Istanbul there is a drab, uninteresting street called Voyvoda Caddesi, where the Turks claim the head is buried. After five centuries it is hardly surprising that Vlad should be the subject of myth, though the archaeologist at Snagov found a crown of white porcelain with blue stones and golden claws of a type awarded to Vlad at a Nuremberg tournament.

The confusion between the historical warrior and Count Dracula is absolute at Bran Castle, where Vlad might have stayed on his various journeys. Today it is referred to brazenly as Castle Dracula or 'Count Dracula's home'. Visually, it fits Stoker's description, impressively high, with small windows in the battlements, turrets and courtyards,

but his fiction is interpreted as fact as guides shuffle through the corridors in the canvas slippers provided at the entrance, repeating the name of Count Dracula in numerous languages.

The Romanian authorities were so appalled by this that they considered building a Castle Dracula in the Borgo Pass to deflect the tourists from Bran and make a fortune from a horror Disneyland, with tapes of howling wolves, befanged waitresses, bats, screams and strange happenings.

In 1972 this horrible idea was just a glimmering, but the Borgo Pass was my final destination and, with unforgotten generosity, the Ministry paid for my journey.

A few days later I woke in the modest little hotel Cerbul in Bistrita, referred to in Stoker's novel as Biztritz, where Jonathan Harker stayed overnight before he left for Castle Dracula. It seemed appropriate that I was roused from my sleep by the sound of hammering; I looked out of the window to see the carpenter opposite hard at work on a coffin.

Returning to Bistrita a few years later, I found a large modern hotel called The Golden Krone, built especially for the Dracula Tours. Their brochure proclaimed: 'Today more than 100 years after the fantastic occurrences related in the pages full of owls, bats, monsters and vampires, the traveller who comes to Bistrita to track down Count Dracula will spend his first night at the same Golden Crown. It has changed a bit, it is a modern hotel built in architectonic style which suggests a medieval burgh.' Bah!

On that first visit, the presence of Dracula was more credible, especially when we drove through the Borgo Pass at dusk with white mists suddenly pierced by a solitary stone cross or the black cloaked figure of a shepherd. The closeness to Stoker's description of Harker setting out for the castle is all the more uncanny because my great-uncle never set foot in Transylvania himself. All he had was an old Baedeker, some photographs of Eastern Europe he saw at a contemporary exhibition in London, and his own imagination.

A few days later we reached the cemetery of Sulina at the mouth of the Danube, and my happy assignment with Death was over.

A Monumental Vanity

I feel uneasy when the going is too good because I smell trouble ahead. And at first it seemed that it was going to be easy to reach Mount Nemrut, instead of the effort I was prepared for.

Arriving at Adiyaman, I made my way to the Antiochus Hotel where the school-teacher was waiting for me as arranged. Explaining our movements for the night ahead, he asked if I would mind sharing a *dolmus* with two Australians, and pointed to a couple sitting outside who looked too old to be Australian.

A shared *dolmus* hardly smacked of adventure, but I said I should be delighted and went over to introduce myself. I tried to be matey, though they did not look particularly matey themselves.

'G'day. How you doing?'

'*Bitte?*' They peered at me suspiciously and I realised the 'Australians' were *Austrians*, the right, elderly age after all. I ate alone, washing a kebab down with a violent little wine called *lav*, named after the lava which poured from the volcano on the label. When I told the schoolteacher that for once I was ready for an early night in order to be prepared for our start, he looked so crestfallen that I allowed him to lead me across a wasteland to his school to show me off to the headmaster, but he came outside again shaking his head: 'Eric, he sleeps.' Lucky Eric, I thought, as we entered the end-of-term embroidery exhibition. For those who like embroidery, this is a sweet occasion with smiling schoolgirls and everyone on their best behaviour. Their handiwork ranged from doilies to the elaborate wedding tent that surrounds a couple when they are at last alone in bed, protecting them from watchful eyes. I was shown every item, introduced to every student, delightfully shy and giggly as I scrutinised the smallest hankie with apparent astonishment, and I realised for the first time what hell the Royal Family must endure with their every reaction observed so carefully. After congratulating everyone on such a first-rate turn-out I returned thankfully to bed.

I was woken at 1.00 a.m. and stumbled downstairs at 1.30 to find the Austrians as bright as babies compared to my bleary self. The teacher was there with his headmaster Eric, who looked little more than seventeen and was yawning hugely. Surprisingly, he had never seen Nemrut before, and had seized the opportunity to join us. The others had finished their glasses of hot, comforting tea, and before I could ask what had happened to mine we were taken to the *dolmus*, which was not the bone-shaking landrover I expected but a respectable Ford station-wagon. So far too good.

Perhaps I should explain why I was anxious to see Mount Nemrut at sunrise. This is the site of one of the strangest man-made follies on earth and I felt it required an effort to go there. Until comparatively recently, nobody did. For two thousand years the ruins had lain untouched until some shepherds and local hunters described them to a German who came to the region at the beginning of the last century. After that, visitors began to make their way laboriously by mule, and even now the road is covered by snow for most of the year and groups are advised go there in July or August. We were early, arriving on 31 May, but the snow had melted.

Shortly before the birth of Christ, Antiochus I erected an extraordinary monument to himself at the top of one of the highest peaks in the kingdom of Commagene, which lay between the River Euphrates and the Taurus Mountains. Here he built his colossal statues of the gods with himself in between. These statues, equalled as far as I know only by those on Easter Island, dominate the eastern terrace above a sacrificial altar; they include Hercules, son of Zeus and the symbol of strength in Greek mythology; Zeus himself, the greatest god of the Greek and Persian religions; Apollo, the apotheosis of the Sun God; and Antiochus himself. This was an act of megalomania in the rare tradition of the Pharaohs. 'I, Antiochus,' he proclaimed, 'caused this monument to be erected in commemoration of my own glory and that of the gods.' Plainly he saw this self-adoration as a divine right, being descended from Alexander the Great on his mother's side, and Darius I of Persia through his father, who was Mithridates I, founder of Commagene.

There are several way of approaching Mount Nemrut. If you come from the opposite direction in the daylight, you will see two considerable landmarks. One is the ancient castle of Eski Kale, memorable for the massive stone relief, which Antiochus erected in memory of his father. Over 100 feet high, it depicts Mithridates shaking hands condescendingly with a short, stout Hercules. If this was a tribute to his father, the Greek inscription was flattering to Antiochus himself, who plainly did not know the meaning of self-doubt. It begins: 'Built by the great king Antiochus, God the Righteous . . .' The relief seems to be in the middle of nowhere yet it remains in remarkable condition – a museum piece without the usual enclosure of a museum. Nearby is the Roman bridge of Cendere, built by the people of Commagene as a tribute, probably exacted, to the Emperor Septimus Severus. It is hard to build an ugly bridge, though rare to find one as graceful as this. As with all truly great architecture, you feel better for seeing it. The proportions are so perfect that ninety-two carved blocks of stone still support a single arch 92 yards long, withstanding the traffic above and the powerful currents of the river Nympheos below. It is a remarkable feat of engineering, as well as an artistic triumph.

Our journey took us 80 kilometres to the village of Khata and the road was then reduced to a bone-shaking track that seemed interminable. Our headlights picked out three rabbits, an emaciated fox and several elegant deer-like dogs which pursued us growling ferociously.

The *dolmus* stopped suddenly and in pitch darkness we began to climb the few hundred yards to the summit. Warned that it would be freezing, I wore an expensive and absurd safari jacket I had bought in London, which now came into its own, buttoned up to the neck. I was thankful for this garment when I saw Eric shuddering from the icy blast, a thin blanket draped across his shoulders.

I should like to say that the ascent was dangerous, but such pretence would be exposed by the many who go to Nemrut today, albeit mostly in the gentler warmth of day. Even so, the track was invisible, with only the teacher's torch to guide us, and the shale made it hard to gain a foothold. Excellent! I thought, as I slipped and hurt my elbow, it is not so easy after all. The wind was so violent it tried to push me over, like an angry opponent, as I tried to stand up.

When we reached the top, nothing was as I had imagined. From the summit of the mountain a tumulus rose a further 50 yards, like a pyramid. This sepulchral mound, which may contain the tomb of Antiochus, has defied every attempt to find the entrance to an inner passage, and the stones tremble warningly when the archaeologists try to excavate, threatening a landslide. No doubt a method will be evolved one day.

As for the statues, they sit in a headless row at the base. Earthquakes, storms, erosion, all the elements have avenged themselves against the mortal insolence that dared to claim equality with the gods. The last head to fall was that of the Goddess of Fortune, which tumbled down in a thunderstorm as recently as 1962.

Curiously, the fact that they are headless does not diminish the statues, especially as the heads have been hoisted upright and look as if they have stood there since the start of time. That of Zeus is supposed to be the largest head in the world, with that of the bearded Antiochus nearby. As if to protect them, they are flanked by eagles and lions, and one magnificent beast appears to be howling his defiance. His was the first outline to emerge that morning, and as it grew lighter I saw the head of the goddess, garlanded with flowers, sprawled on the ground near me. The first steps of the sacrificial altar lay beyond her.

The wind was still so violent that I sheltered behind a wall, thinking, as I have done so often before, that the hour before the dawn is the most dismal. Gradually I sensed the immensity of the view below us, with the faint ribbon of the Euphrates meandering into the distance. The scale was eerie and I wondered how Antiochus was able to build here. An army of ant-like slaves dragged the blocks of marble for the statues from Gerger, 30 kilometres away, while the black marble used for the reliefs at the base of the tumulus

was carried from the eastern quarry of Karabalen.

It was easy to understand why Antiochus chose such a prominence, for he was looking down on all Mesopotamia. Once so fruitful, now so barren, it is soon to be revived by another man-made wonder – one of the greatest irrigation schemes ever known, which will divert the Tigris and Euphrates, creating a lake so large that it will change the climate.

How long it took the sun to rise. I moved behind the head of a god to be ready with my camera the moment it appeared, my fingers trembling in the cold as I tried to set the exposure in advance.

And then the sun came up.

I suppose I gasped. It was neither black nor green, as I had been told, but a molten explosion which gave the impression of a raw-red force pushed from the centre of the earth as if the core had shattered. I now knew why Antiochus had placed his Gods in this direction, as if in obeisance. If a man had never seen this sunrise before he might have fallen on his knees in fear of what might follow.

I could see the sun throb and wondered why I could not hear it. Then suddenly it was torn from the earth and became familiar as it entered the sky. The ascent cannot have lasted more than fifteen seconds. It was rising rapidly now, growing paler, the fury over, and I was left below for a few ecstatic moments more, shaking with excitement.

Antiochus' boast that 'no living human being shall be able to build anything higher than this shrine' has long since been refuted, but I could only marvel at his audacity. This was beyond vanity.

I came back to earth. The wind dropped and the day grew hot, though it was barely seven in the morning. As we descended I asked the teacher if we could stop at an open-air *lokanta* for tea. None was forthcoming. In a country where tea is almost compulsory, this made no sense.

Stopping at the bridge of Cendere, I walked to another *lokanta* and asked for *chai* with a beaming smile, thirsty and virtuous after the night's vigil. A charade ensued with the promise of hot water instead. When no hot water arrived, the obvious struck me at last – this was the first day of Ramadan, the fast which is so absolute in the East that Turks run the risk of being stoned if they drink from a fountain in the daytime.

The news galvanised the Austrians for the first time. 'This is not bloody good enough,' the husband shouted at the schoolteacher in English, presumably for my benefit. 'Ramadan for you, but why for us? Very good. We declare our own Ramadan – we pay half-price for *dolmus* because there is no tea.'

The wretched teacher who was hoping for a tip looked mortified, Eric was oblivious, I was parched.

As the Austrian sat back triumphantly his wife addressed me for the first time. Until then she had made no comment on anything, not even on Mount Nemrut, having stayed in the station-wagon throughout.

'Be sure,' she advised me, her face brightening with pleasure, 'when we come back to Adiyaman, to go to the *lycée*. They have there this exhibition of embroideries. Now *that* is lovely!'

The Gorge of Samaria

The approach was good: I left Chania in the north-west of Crete at nine in the morning, reaching Omolos an hour and a half later. At first there were gnarled olive trees, and then the bus climbed through orange groves bright with fruit, the blue sea behind us and pine-covered mountains ahead. The peaks were still covered with drifts of snow though this was a hot day in May.

At first the walk was deceptive, zig-zagging gently beside a river that leapt from one dazzling pool to another. A notice at the top warned me that swimming was at one's own risk, but the pools looked so pure that I could not resist plunging naked into one of the deepest; the impact of icy water cleared my head sensationally. The notice also warned me not to fish, shoot, trap, scream or make loud noises. For once there was not a transistor to be heard, only a few faint voices in the distance, and the sound of the rustling water and the wind in the cypress trees, infinitely restful after the cheerful din of Chania's harbour, where motor-bikes screeched at random.

Halfway down I paused among the ruins of the old city of Samaria, set on a plateau of lush exotic plants where the stillness was almost sinister. The descent began to grow more formidable as the gorge narrowed. Until then, I had jumped merrily over boulders to cross the river. Now, swollen by the melted snow, it became wilder and suddenly all sunlight was excluded.

Robert Pashley, one of the earliest explorers of the gorge, ascended from the other direction and described it in 1837 as 'the grandest and at the same time the most picturesque spot on the island'. He had the assistance of a mule, but he conceded that 'the path in some parts is so narrow round the abrupt precipices that no horse would be able

to pass along it'. At the Gates, where the 'lofty chasm' is ten feet across at the ground, widening to about thirty or forty at the top, it was necessary to pass 'in the middle of the rapid stream . . . and for a hundred paces further we are more in the water than out of it, having to cross the torrent several times.'

Descending from the north without a mule, my experience was similar. Time and time again I had to wade through the swirling water, shoes, trousers and camera held as high as possible. The thought of turning back was tempting but a sense of English honour spurred me on. At moments I had to cling on to any crevices in the rock to save myself from being swept away, between alarming scrambles over faces of rock.

I remembered that the notice at the top warned one against attempting the gorge on one's own, and I was starting to think myself one-hell-of-a-fellow, overtaking a group of Germans tied together with ropes and fully equipped with alpenstocks, until I was joined by a group of elderly French ladies from the Touring Club of France who swam past with the serenity of swans.

The descent should have taken five hours, but due to the melting snow and swollen waters I emerged at the beach near Haghia Roumeli on the other side of Crete eight hours later, as darkness was beginning to fall.

There were several concrete huts 'to let' where I could spend the night, for the linking boat had grown tired of waiting for stragglers. As I entered a barrack-like room for dinner, the Germans were chomping away, flushed with triumph, swilling beer, singing loudly, while the French ladies, only slightly dishevelled, kept themselves apart. They recognised me and called me over with cries of '*Entente cordiale!*' in the brief camaraderie of shared experience; how well I slept.

It is no great achievement to walk down the Gorge of Samaria and I imagine that thousands do so today, though it was closed for several months when two Britons were drowned in a 'flash flood' which swept down the gorge in October 1988. Both men were travelling alone.

Conclusion

Risk and effort add to the zest of travel, yet the most modest of journeys can be rewarding, be it a trip to Blackpool or Frinton-on-Sea. One of the happiest I have known recently was hardly off the beaten track – Easter in Paris in 1988.

Paris is a first love. I had headed there from Frankfurt when I was discharged from the American army and I toured the stage-set stalls of the flea market with my Rolleiflex.

I had been there since, but this was my first visit for many years and I dreaded finding that Paris had changed as sadly as London. Instead, I found the opposite was true. The old buildings seemed lovelier, the stone more mellow, the views across the Seine still open with only an occasional tower block in the distance, unlike the combination of blitzed building-sites and soaring towers of modern London.

On a warm, crisp morning as the mist started to rise I walked over the Pont Royal from the Left Bank, and across the Tuileries Gardens towards the Obelisk of Luxor with the roar of the Champs-Elysées beyond, in order to visit the Musée de l'Orangerie and the circular room downstairs which is lined with Monet's final obsession – his water-lilies. Photographs I had seen had not prepared me for that flesh-tingling sensation when you are confronted with something that makes you suddenly, gloriously, thankful to be alive. I emerged as refreshed as if I had plunged into one of the pools in the Gorge of Samaria, and headed for my first sidewalk drink of the day – *entente cordiale* again. That Easter was enriched by the great exhibition of Van Gogh in the astonishing setting of the d'Orsay, the former railway station; the Degas at the Grand Palais; and my first visit to the Rodin Museum in the Hotel de Biron, the *Penseur* contemplating in the garden outside, and Rodin's bust of a *Young Girl Wearing a Hat Adorned with*

Roses inside, as free and light as air, teaching me that sculpture can be spontaneous.

As one grows older, art is another excuse for travel, and I respect those elderly ladies who dismount from their coaches and set up their easels in some Italian town. It is possible to lead a perfectly honourable life without leaving one's own doorstep, but as we have the luck to be born into this strange, varied world, it seems a shame not to see as much of it as possible.

I was reminded of how limitless horizons can be when Anthony Eyers, the editor of *Isis*, came to see me in the spring of 1989. His wanderlust made my own seem mundane. He had driven across the Sahara with friends; now he intended to cross China in search of lobster.

'Lobster!' I echoed, thinking of that vast hinterland. 'In China?'

'China has a massive coastline, too,' he responded. 'I bet the lobsters are jolly good!'

Here was a traveller indeed, but what was the spur that urged him on, why did he travel? He gave me a marvellous answer: 'To get rid of my preconceptions.'

That is what travel is all about. Life itself, for that matter.

The trouble is that so many people *want* to find their preconceptions when they go abroad. On a recent flight to Istanbul, the plane was partly filled with English football supporters, unmistakable with their tiny Union Jack hats, bare midriffs and beer cans. They were fun and treated me as a curiosity.

'Bet he's loaded,' said one, giving me the nickname of 'Billy Bundles'. At that moment, the plane dipped and he called to the others: 'Billy Bundles has just dropped his wallet!' Everyone laughed, myself included.

But when I asked what they hoped to see in Istanbul, their mood changed.

'Howderyermean?' asked one suspiciously.

With staggering naïvety I suggested a trip down the Bosphorus or a visit to the Topkapi. The stupidity was mine.

'Nah.' He scowled. 'We've come to get legless, haven't we.' For a moment he brightened: 'Tell us where we can get some birds. That's all we want, booze and birds.'

'There's a nice local drink call *raki*,' I said, 'but the girls may be difficult unless you find a brothel.'

Word must have gone ahead, for they were penned behind glass when I saw them last, to be shunted directly to Izmir where the match was taking place – that city's loss, though Istanbul's gain. From behind the glass came the faint refrain: "Ere we go, 'ere we go . . .' But even when they were released I doubted if they were going anywhere. There was nothing reprehensible in their attitude; it just seemed a waste to go so far and see so little.

It was not their intention to *travel* – all they wanted was a good time. Why should I expect a purpose which never occurred to them; they were simply going to a football match.

'Travelling is Victory!' wrote Conrad, emulating an Arab proverb, but he travelled when the going was tough and depended on the traveller rather than the agency. He could hardly fail to encounter new experience. Today the TV camera penetrates to the heart of darkness to film the pert presenter in Africa '*au naturelle*'. Yet the exploration is passive, almost negative. Holiday by holiday, the programmes wipe out the unspoilt places in the world like bulldozers clearing a rain-forest, except that they destroy with platitudes:

> Andy: Tell me, Amanda, Figmentora isn't too foreign is it?
>
> Amanda: I'm glad you asked me that, Andy. In case anyone's worried, you can have the old kebab if you're brave enough to venture into a side-street, otherwise, rest assured, it's good old British fare back in the hotel where lunch for 2,000 always has chips for the kids. One thing Morocco has in common is a nice cuppa. They like it minty, but you can get P.G. Tips too.
>
> Andy: That's a relief!
>
> Amanda: I thought it might be! As for fish, Captain Birdseye eat your heart out! One word of warning, Andy, there are places which are so quiet you can hear the click of the lace-maker's needles.
>
> Andy: Oh, lord!
>
> Amanda: But if you're rarin' to go and find happiness at the end of your particular rainbow, the pool is the place to check out the talent and flaunt your new outfit. Could bruise your pocket, but it's sheer magic!
>
> Andy: Amanda, are you being goosed or do you want to go to the loo?
>
> Amanda: Gosh!
>
> Andy: Because that's the impression you give, unless you're going mad.
>
> Amanda: N-D-ARMO! That's Italian for 'make tracks'! Next week, see you from Silesia.

A TV 'travel experience' is a tutti-frutti ice-cream. Today there are tourists and holiday-makers and just a few genuine travellers. I wish I could count myself among the latter, and may yet prove I can.

Meanwhile, returning to my home in North Devon at the end of a radiant April day, the train passed through the English countryside, which seemed as unchanged as a background by Stubbs. I know of few views more satisfying than looking across the estuary of the Taw and Torridge Rivers, towards the hills of Exmoor in the far distance, yet, perversely, this morning the water shimmered so deceptively, so beckoningly, that I yearned to be off again to a warmer, less polluted sea. Perhaps again to Thassos, for the first of May is near.